The Ancient Path

ALSO BY JOCELYN DROZDA

Candy For Breakfast

———

Invisible No More: Answering the Call to Arms
Book I - Healing Relational Perspective

———

Invisible No More: Answering the Call to Arms
Book II - Personal Identity Restored

———

Invisible No More: Answering the Call to Arms
Book III - Identity in Christ: Aligned with Destiny

———

———◆———

Coming Soon ...

Draw Your Sword: Stories from the Battle
Take Wing

The Ancient Path

Unraveling the Mystery of Divine Guidance

Jocelyn Anne Drozda
M.Ed, B.Ed

Helena, Montana

Ahelia Publishing

The Ancient Path: Unraveling the Mystery of Divine Guidance

Ahelia Publishing

The Memorial Stones

4 And it came to pass, when all the people had completely crossed over the Jordan, that the Lord spoke to Joshua, saying: **2** "Take for yourselves twelve men from the people, one man from every tribe, **3** and command them, saying, 'Take for yourselves twelve stones from here, out of the midst of the Jordan, from the place where the priests' feet stood firm. You shall carry them over with you and leave them in the lodging place where you lodge tonight.' " **4** Then Joshua called the twelve men whom he had appointed from the children of Israel, one man from every tribe; **5** and Joshua said to them: "Cross over before the ark of the Lord your God into the midst of the Jordan, and each one of you take up a stone on his shoulder, according to the number of the tribes of the children of Israel, **6** that this may be a sign among you when your children ask in time to come, saying, 'What do these stones *mean* to you?'

7 Then you shall answer them that the waters of the Jordan were cut off before the ark of the covenant of the Lord; when it crossed over the Jordan, the waters of the Jordan were cut off. And these stones shall be for a memorial to the children of Israel forever." **8** And the children of Israel did so, just as Joshua commanded, and took up twelve stones from the midst of the Jordan, as the Lord had spoken to Joshua, according to the number of the tribes of the children of Israel, and carried them over with them to the place where they lodged, and laid them down there. **9** Then Joshua set up twelve stones in the midst of the Jordan, in the place where the feet of the priests who bore the ark of the covenant stood; and they are there to this day.

Joshua 4:1-9

Dedication

This book is dedicated to Tara Yemba and Ruebi Erfle, whose acts of obedience ushered me onto the ancient path my feet were to tread.

Prophetic Word–March 2018

I saw a paper with handwriting on it, but when I looked at it I couldn't understand what was written. It was like it was a different language. I feel that God has given you the gift of translating Him for other people. They may hear God's voice; they may see His hand in their lives, but they don't understand what is going on. They don't know where He is. They cry out for Him and they don't understand He is there because they can't read Him—they don't understand what to look for.

But through the valleys, through the walk you have been on, God has empowered you and given you this ability to translate Him and to translate Him to other people so they can see how much they are loved; so they can receive healing and guidance from Him …

— Bente Thakre

Contents

MY HEART TO YOURS

I am in the process of painting the main space of my house. I did not especially want to take the time nor bear the expense, but it is like I can no longer breathe within its confines. When I first moved in, the colors were pale—making my small house too expansive to feel safe. I didn't understand my color choices at the time but just knew I needed the walls to hug me a little tighter.

Now I understand them. The sage green that became the color of the living room was for my healing. The bright gold hallway next to the rust-red accent wall signaled I was in the refiner's fire and would be for the next ten years. I don't even like those colors. My daughter unaffectionately called it "The Hot Dog House." The burgundy of my bedroom covered me with the Blood of Jesus as I journeyed through the valleys and into the foothills.

I understood a new season was finally on the horizon when the Lord asked me to give away all the word paintings I had created during my time of healing. I no longer needed them, and I was to pass them on to The Ones who did. He was taking me out of the fire. Now, as I rest here in transition between the old and the new, my walls are also in transition. This was to be my prophetic declaration of stepping into a new place in my life. Sky blue. *The breath of God. Holy Spirit.* The color of *ascent*, and being seated in *heavenly places.*[1] This is to where the Lord is calling me—calling you.

These are the stories of my journey that taught me to be sensitive to the voice of God and follow His divine leading. They tell of how I learned to be ever aware of His presence—to be ever aware of His guiding Hand as He led me through the darkness along the ancient path. I no longer believe in coincidence; significance is revealed in hindsight. I share my journey at the request of the Lord not to be replicated, as each of our paths and relationship with Him will be as unique as we are, but to show you what it looked like for me from a practical rather than theological perspective. In doing so, I pray you recognize His divine guidance in ways that may have previously escaped notice, unraveling some of the mystery of walking with the Lord.

May God bless you as you become ever aware of His presence and guidance as you seek the ancient path.

Jocelyn Anne Drozda

As for me, I will see Your face in
righteousness; I shall be satisfied
when I awake in Your likeness.
Psalm 17:15

PART ONE

SETTING OUT

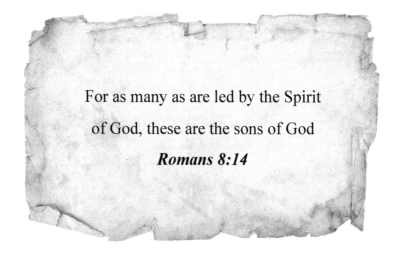

For as many as are led by the Spirit

of God, these are the sons of God

Romans 8:14

1. CATCH THE CURRENT

Enter by the narrow gate. For the gate
is wide and the way is easy that leads
to destruction, and those who enter by
it are many. For the gate is narrow
and the way is hard that leads to life,
and those who find it are few.

Matthew 7:13-14 (ESV)

You make known to me the path of
life; in your presence there is fullness
of joy; at your right hand are pleasures
forevermore.

Psalm 16:11 (ESV)

Strategy to Implement

**Choose the narrow gate and
open yourself up to walking in His ways.**

Paddles resting lazily across the bow of the boat, we laid back, enjoying the sunshine, scenery, and the relaxed pace of *The Float Down the River*. This has become an annual event for many at LifeLinks International Family Camp, held in Montana every summer. We launch the fleet of boats on the river behind the grounds and debark at a specified location down the river, where we had strategically parked enough vehicles to carpool back to camp.

Along the river route one can hear the laughter, splashing, exhilarated shouts, and other such sounds of fun. There is no striving involved, other than redirecting to descend down a side channel, navigate your way out of a whirlpool, or to avoid the occasional rock wall or overhanging branch. It makes all the difference when you catch the current.

Once caught up in a current, it is exponentially difficult to extract ourselves from it or to go in another direction—making it crucial to ensure we are in a current that will lead us exactly where we need to go. We often do not recognize we are being propelled in the wrong direction until desolation lies as evidence all around us. Yet we do not have to choose the current of the ways of the world—the wide path that leads to destruction. God has provided another current that leads to *life*. It is harder to find, but once we are in its midst, it is powerful beyond imagination. This current, called "walking in the Spirit," empowers us to receive divine guidance at levels far above what many of us expect or experience.

As I look back over my thirty-plus-year-walk as a Christian, I can see God's guiding hand in my life; I was just not truly aware of the depth of it at the time—*for the first twenty-six years!* How did that happen? How did I not discover or learn the available depth of walking in the Spirit but was, rather, *barely aware* of its existence? How did I not understand I could hear the voice of the Lord so loudly it would not only guide me to, but lead me through each intricate twist and turn on the path of my journey? The answer is simple. I had not found the ancient path.

Perhaps it was because I did not understand what walking with God looked like, or how it worked—it was not directly taught in a practical sense in any of the settings I found myself. I now know the information was available, and it was practiced in some churches; it had just not come across my path in such a way that I could fully grasp it; nor had I actively pursued it.

Another factor of my ignorance, and I am sure this plagues many of us, was that it required more of an investment of time, energy, and resources than I was prepared to surrender at the time—

not to mention the necessary risk and discomfort. We must determine the expenditure to be worthwhile—a Matthew 13: *sell all you have and buy the field* type of investment.

The Parable of the Hidden Treasure

The kingdom of heaven is like a treasure hidden in a field, which a man found and covered up. Then in his joy he goes and sells all that he has and buys that field.

Matthew 13:44 (ESV)

The deep mysteries of the Lord are released and entrusted into the hands of those who treasure the time spent at His feet in the secret place, tucked away from the distractions and distortions of the world. Corporate worship and prayer are valuable, but *nothing* replaces time spent alone with the Lord.

A third obstacle was insufficient **trust** and **faith** on my part. I did not understand I could trust Him with every facet of my life, nor did I believe He would concern Himself with me to that degree. I did not have the knowledge nor the faith to believe that as I learned to actively listen, I could hear the voice of God to such minute specifications; He is exceedingly capable of making Himself clearly heard and understood. Instead, I fell prey to the lies that mocked me: *It was just coincidence. You're just imagining it all. You are inventing it in your own mind.* Or the best one of all, *Who do you think you are that God would talk to you?*

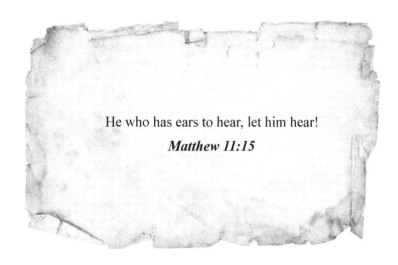

He who has ears to hear, let him hear!
Matthew 11:15

19

The Ancient Path

A further deterrent, and perhaps the hardest to overcome, was that following God's leading required the complete surrender of my will and agenda; I had to give up control of my life. I could no longer pursue what I wanted, when I wanted, and do what I could to achieve it. I believed that if I followed God with my whole heart, He would make me do things I didn't want to do, and I would miss out on my dreams.

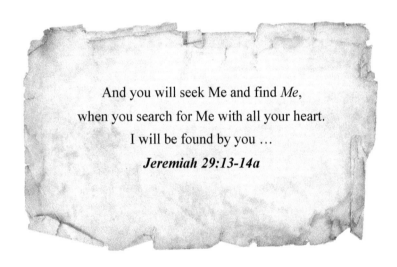

And you will seek Me and find *Me*,
when you search for Me with all your heart.
I will be found by you ...
Jeremiah 29:13-14a

Yes, in fact, He did (and continues to) *ask* me to do things I do not wish to do, but as I stepped out in obedience, I realized that all the things I didn't want to do because of different variations of fear were actually holding me back from my passions and dreams—the

The Ancient Path

very same passions and dreams God Himself placed in my heart. It was in doing those very things I didn't want to do that helped me grow in the depth of character, courage, faith, strength, and spiritual stamina needed to carry the destiny God had designed for me. (No wonder the enemy did not want me doing them!)

As I exchanged *fear of man* deposited in my heart by the enemy with *fear of the Lord* (reverence for His majesty and a deep desire to please Him above man), I began to understand that in His love for me, God created me with unique purposes. It is only when I am walking in those purposes—the ones that tap into the passions of my heart—and in close relationship with Him, *that* I live in the fullness of joy and peace, despite outward circumstances. And I can only walk that path when He is beside me, leading my steps, for it is not easy. As you start walking the ancient path in complete surrender to His designs, you also realize that putting your life in His hands, the One who already knows the whole story, with *all* its volumes, is unequivocally the best possible choice in every circumstance!

Catch the current! It makes all the difference. Let's pray. Come, Holy Spirit, we invite You.

[Pray each prayer out loud. They are not merely words on a page; there is power in the spoken word. Adapt, change, add to each prayer, whatever you feel is applicable to your unique situation, and as you feel led.]

The Ancient Path

Dear Lord,

Thank You for making known to me the path of life. Thank You that in Your presence is fullness of joy, and at Your right hand are pleasures forevermore. Teach me the mysteries of walking with You, in the depth of Your presence. Help me to seek You with all of my heart. In doing so, according to Your Word, I know You will be found. Help me to spend time at Your feet in the secret place so I may come to know You. I want to *know* You, Father God. I want to *know* You, Lord Jesus. I want to *know* You, precious Holy Spirit. I am answering Your call to be seated in heavenly places. Teach me to be sensitive to Your voice so You can lead me where I need to be. Lead me through the darkness into Your great light, and tell me the great and hidden things.

Lead me to the narrow gate, O Lord, and help me to walk on its ancient path. I choose the narrow gate! I choose Your life for me! Help me to walk away from the easier ways of the world. Keep me and my loved ones off of the wide path that leads to destruction. Help me to walk in the Spirit each and every moment, empowering me to receive divine guidance.

Forgive me, Lord, for not investing the needed time, energy, and resources to learn to hear Your voice and to follow You with every part of me. I repent for not having the trust and faith I need to know You are speaking, always speaking to me, and that I can hear Your voice—You *will* teach me. I repent for any times I passed off Your voice as a coincidence or my imagination, when it was, in fact, You speaking to me.

Help me to surrender my agenda and my will completely, giving up control of my life, so You can take control. I want to follow Your ways—the ancient path. I come out of alignment with fear from the enemy that has held me back. Help me grow in depth of character, courage, faith, strength, and spiritual stamina I need to carry the destiny You have designed for me. I ask for the fear of man to be replaced with the fear of the Lord. I ask for the grace by which I may serve You acceptably with reverence and godly fear. I pray this in the name of the Lord Jesus Christ. Amen.

Who *is* the man that fears the LORD? Him shall He teach in the way He chooses. He himself shall dwell in prosperity, And his descendants shall inherit the earth. The secret of the LORD *is* with those who fear Him, And He will show them His covenant. My eyes *are* ever toward the LORD, For He shall pluck my feet out of the net.

Psalm 25:12-15

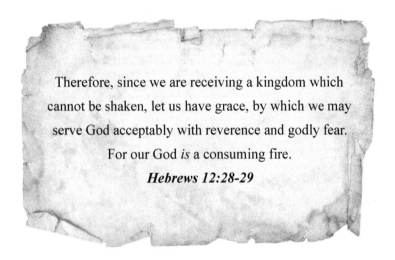

Therefore, since we are receiving a kingdom which cannot be shaken, let us have grace, by which we may serve God acceptably with reverence and godly fear. For our God *is* a consuming fire.

Hebrews 12:28-29

Connect the Dots:

Ask the Lord God if there is anything else you need to bring before Him at this time. Ask if there is anything He would have you do.

(Sit quietly before Him. If anything else comes to your mind, pray about it. Record any insights. It is much easier to "Connect the Dots" when they are written out and you can refer back to them. Follow through on any directives He gives you. The following are possible methods to expand your time and intentionality as you commune with the Lord after you read each chapter.

The Ancient Path

Do you need to reread or highlight any particular sections of this chapter? Ask the Lord why they are significant to you. Is there a specific response required? Are there any questions forming in your mind? Write them down. Leave space after them to record anything the Lord brings to your attention that shows you the answer or leads you to answers. This may come in the form of Scripture, another written, oral, or visual source, from another person, dropped directly into your spirit, or from another incredibly creative God-source.

Make time to read the rest of the chapter for several of the given Scriptures. Record any words or phrases that stand out to you. Look up their definitions. Do a further study on any concepts which seem significant, or about which you have questions. Write down any insights or understandings that form as you read, or that you discover later through any source.)

_____

_____

_____

_____

_____

_____

The Ancient Path

_____

_____

_____

_____

_____

_____

_____

_____

_____

_____

_____

_____

_____

_____

_____

_____

_____

2. JONES MINUS THE HAT

Then Gideon said to God, "If you will save Israel by my hand, as you have said, behold, I am laying a fleece of wool on the threshing floor. If there is dew on the fleece alone, and it is dry on all the ground, then I shall know that you will save Israel by my hand, as you have said." And it was so. When he rose early next morning and squeezed the fleece, he wrung enough dew from the fleece to fill a bowl with water. Then Gideon said to God, "Let not your anger burn against me; let me speak just once more. Please let me test just once more with the fleece. Please let it be dry on the fleece only, and on all the ground let there be dew." And God did so that night; and it was dry on the fleece only, and on all the ground there was dew.

Judges 6:36-40 (ESV)

Strategy to Implement

Ask the Lord for a sign.
He wants to lead you into His purposes.

I often feel like a female version of Indiana Jones. I have found divine guidance to be much like a quest for treasure, with hints and clues and mysteries all woven together, just beckoning for me to follow the threads and unravel them. My life became an interactive adventure with God once I became aware of how to read the signs and understood my role in the unfolding saga.

Signs from our creative God can come in endless variation and form, many not yet experienced. We are familiar with the big ones —the star, the rainbow, fire falling from Heaven—signs for nations, people groups, and for the whole world to see. Yet somehow, when He gives us the little ones *just for us*, we don't believe they are from the Lord, or we pass them off as coincidence. Just like Graham Cooke indicates somewhere in the vast oceans of his teachings, God doesn't write a book and then forget how to speak! Under the same principle, God doesn't communicate through signs for centuries, then put them aside.

The Ancient Path

Perhaps the lack of faith stems from the disbelief that the Lord of all Heaven and Earth would concern Himself with each individual. However, Luke 12:7 reminds us the very hairs on our head are numbered, and we are of more value than many sparrows. He knows us to the depth of our being and thinks about us again and again. (It is a *remarkable truth*, isn't it!)

> And in Your book they all were written,
> The days fashioned for me,
> When as *yet there were* none of them.
> How precious also are Your thoughts to me, O God!
> How great is the sum of them!
> *If* I should count them, they would be more
> in number than the sand …
> *Psalm 139:16b-18a*

If we truly understand our identity in Christ as a much loved child of God and of great value to Him, just to start with, we would fully comprehend that yes, He does *more* than take the time and make the effort to correspond with us. In fact, He communicates with us for the purpose of drawing us into an intimate relationship

The Ancient Path

with Him. That's what it is all about; that is what everything is about —intimacy in relationship with Him. And through that intimacy and time with Him, we become more and more like Him, reflecting His character as we are sanctified and become vessels fit for His service.

God strategically places messages in our midst to catch our attention, prompting us to engage with Him, ask questions, converse, and respond in ways that will move us and those connected to us further along in our journey. It is sad that many of us, including myself, have had our heads so deeply buried in fabricated distractions, misplaced priorities, and organized chaos that we are not aware of (or we even consciously step over) the treasures of communication from the Lord falling around us and lying at our feet. Perhaps we have confused *receiving signs* with *demanding signs*, knowing we should not put the Lord to test, and this somehow nullifies the idea that He sends them to us.

But He sighed deeply in His spirit, and said, "Why does this generation seek a sign? Assuredly, I say to you, no sign will be given to this generation."
Mark 8:12

Others, testing *Him*, sought from Him a sign from heaven.
Luke 11:16

The Ancient Path

However, if we examine the Scriptures such as found in Mark and Luke, they are in context of the Pharisees and others demanding a sign from Jesus to prove He is God. We can contrast this with the event as recounted in Judges 6, where Gideon not only asked for a specific sign, but did so *twice* for the same situation. The difference is in the heart attitude and motivation. There was no seeking of personal glory or recognition for Gideon. He was not attempting to manipulate God in any manner. Gideon truly desired to know the heart of the Father and wanted his actions to be in obedience to God's will, and was therefore taking no chances. God was more than willing to answer Gideon's query with a sign ... or two!

There is also much scriptural evidence of the Lord interacting with His people through signs. We are both encouraged to ask the Lord for signs, and informed that God gives signs to demonstrate His faithfulness. The Scriptures indicate signs were given to guide actions, and that we are to use His Word as a sign to us.

And these words which I command you today shall be in your heart. You shall teach them diligently to your children, and shall talk of them when you walk by the way, when you lie down, and when you rise up. You shall bind them as a sign on your hand, and they shall be as frontlets between your eyes.

Deuteronomy 6:6-8

The Ancient Path

And this *is* the sign to you from the LORD, that the LORD will do this thing which He has spoken: Behold, I will bring the shadow on the sundial, which has gone down with the sun on the sundial of Ahaz, ten degrees backward." So the sun returned ten degrees on the dial by which it had gone down.

Isaiah 38:7-8

And let it be, when these signs come to you, *that* you do as the occasion demands; for God *is* with you.

1 Samuel 10:7

And he said to him, "If now I have found favor in your eyes, then show me a sign that it is you who speak with me.

Judges 6:17 (ESV)

The blood shall be a sign for you, on the houses where you are. And when I see the blood, I will pass over you, and no plague will befall you to destroy you, when I strike the land of Egypt.
Exodus12:13 (ESV)

Show me a sign of your favor, that those who hate me may see and be put to shame because you, LORD, have helped me and comforted me.
Psalm 86:17 (ESV)

Instead of the thorn shall come up the cypress tree, And instead of the briar shall come up the myrtle tree; And it shall be to the LORD for a name, for an everlasting sign *that* shall not be cut off."
Isaiah 55:13

Now, Lord, look on their threats, and grant to Your servants
that with all boldness they may speak Your word, by
stretching out Your hand to heal, and that signs and wonders
may be done through the name of Your holy Servant Jesus.

Acts 4:29-30

"Ask a sign of the LORD your God; let it

be deep as Sheol or high as heaven."

Isaiah 7:11 (ESV)

The danger, where we must not allow our feet to tread, is to seek the signs of God in and of themselves, rather than seeking Jesus. Signs and the power of God are fascinating; it is natural to be intrigued, but everything should flow out of an intimate relationship with Him, not out of an enthrallment with the supernatural.

Journal entry - January 2016

Lord, I want all You have for me, but don't let me get caught up in that, let me only be caught up in You! Help me keep my eyes fixed on You and You alone! Walk with me!

As you spend time with Jesus over the next few weeks, consider putting all disbelief on the shelf, and instead assuming that *everything* happening around you is significant. From that state of openness, the Lord can guide you into which threads you need to unravel. Approach this journey with a heart of *anticipation* and *expectancy.* Believe that you will find the treasures He has so carefully laid out for you … and you will. Come, pray with me as the Lord opens the new book of your life, and you begin your journey on the ancient path of ascension.

The Ancient Path

Heavenly Father,

I stand before You as a much loved child of God—Your much loved child. Thank you that I am highly valued by You—the Creator of the heavens and the earth. I am ready to embark on an adventure with You. Teach me who I am. Teach me who You are.

I repent for believing You don't value me enough to bother with me or to speak with me. That is contrary to Your Word. Let me hear Your voice more and more clearly every day! Let me become ever aware of the signs and messages You put before me, and bring me into an understanding of them. I repent for allowing myself to be pulled away from You and Your path for me by the distractions of the world. Help me to fully engage with You, prioritizing the things in my life and disbanding the chaos of my world so I can develop the relationship with You I need to have and You desire to have.

I long for an intimate relationship with You, Lord. Draw me into Your presence. I want to become like You, reflecting more and more of Your character. Help me to become a sanctified vessel, fit for Your service.

Throughout my journey, help me to continually seek You, not the things of You, increasing my discernment so I will always see and understand the difference. Put a sense of expectancy and anticipation into my heart as I lay it bare before You, O Lord. Open my soul to Your ways as we open the new book of my life and begin to walk this road together. I pray this in Jesus' name. Amen.

The Ancient Path

Connect the Dots:

_____

_____

_____

_____

_____

_____

_____

_____

_____

_____

_____

_____

_____

_____

_____

_____

3. HERDING KITTENS

I fed you with milk and not with solid
food; for until now you were not able
to *receive it*, and even now you are
still not able …

1 Corinthians 3:2

If you have run with the footmen, and
they have wearied you, Then how can you
contend with horses? And *if* in the land of
peace, *In which* you trusted, *they wearied
you*, Then how will you do
in the floodplain of the Jordan?

Jeremiah 12:5

Strategy to Implement

Learn to hear from the Lord for yourself; stop depending on others for direction and discernment.

God called me to be a warrior. It was *almost* audible—shockingly clear and so out of context I knew it had to be Him. At the time I was anything but—still hiding in my victim mentality, feeling weak, weary, lost, alone, and afraid. I couldn't fight for myself, let alone for others. It wasn't long after, that my friend handed me Graham Cooke's *The Way of the Warrior*[2] series. The light went on in two different fronts: there was supposed to be more to me than was currently expressed, and *the Lord was definitely trying to tell me something.*

Though I may not have "connected the dots" at the time, in reflection, it is one of the earliest recollections I have of when God extended to me an invitation to come explore with Him and see what He might tell me. There comes a time in our walk of faith that we have to stop depending on others for discernment and direction. We have to learn for ourselves how to be led and fed by the Lord. We need to stop being among the kittens that need to be herded and learn to run with the stallions.

I had reached that point. I wanted to arise, strong and bold, and be drafted into the Lord's army, taking my place on the front lines. I therefore had to know for myself what He wanted me to do, when He wanted me to do it. Though I could and still can benefit from what other people had learned from the Lord, I needed to know for myself what He would ask *of me*.

This required a shift in my priorities, moving *time in His presence* to the forefront. It was that simple. (Don't confuse simple, however, with easy!) Time in His presence … everything else flows out of *time in His presence*. This is where you begin to know His heart for you and for others. This is where you learn to partner with Him to move mountains. And this is where you fall in love with His goodness, His mercy, His grace—all of Him.

Since that initial tentative expedition of what it meant to be a warrior and how it could come to be in one such as me, I have become ever aware of His hand in my life. And as I laid at His feet each day, I began noticing how often "coincidences" would occur around me and in connection with others also seeking His face. Key images and words or phrases would resonate in my soul as I read His Word and looked around me—things I had never taken notice of before, and would not have uncovered had I not taken the time in His presence to listen—then I would hear or see them repeated, once, twice or more, eventually formulating an understanding that I was to take some sort of action in response. Or perhaps the same Scripture would be given to three of us in separate manners within a twenty-four hour period; or the same prophetic picture would be presented by separate people, confirming without a doubt whatever the Lord was telling me at the time, and thus directing my steps.

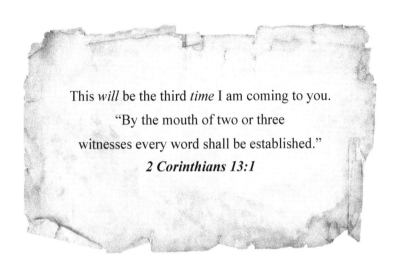

This *will* be the third *time* I am coming to you. "By the mouth of two or three witnesses every word shall be established."
2 Corinthians 13:1

My journal became a critical tool on my journey, allowing me to look back at such things as revelations and insights, the cries of my heart as I prayed in desperation, what had been spoken and prayed over me, things I had read or seen that touched my spirit, what the Lord had spoken to my heart, which Scriptures had started burning in my chest or had been given to me through others ... an endless list. With the "dots" recorded in black and white (and green, blue, and red), it was exceedingly easier to connect them! There are still numerous times He leads me back to a specific journal and gently reminds me, "Remember, this is what I have said." Sometimes the timing of the action He requires me to take is only when I glance back at an old journal, months or even several years later. It is amazing how what seems so random can be so specific as He leads me to a previous entry.

As God led me on that rocky, uphill path of following Him, treacherous at times, I grew to trust that I was hearing His voice and that He would be faithful to guide me as I obediently walked in step with Him.

Prophetic word - September 2018

I feel that the Lord is saying that you have the heart of Mary … that you are one who would sit at the feet of Jesus and that you would pour out whatever it is that you could find in yourself to give to Him. But more than just do it once … even when you feel empty, that you would do that and He wants you to know that He is honored by that kind of heart.

—Rebecca King

Come, Holy Spirit, as we pray together.

The Ancient Path

Thank you, Lord, that the time is now! I accept Your gracious invitation to explore new territory with You, and see what You might tell me. I *want* to be the warrior You have called me to be—one who can contend with horses. I want to arise, strong and bold, and be drafted into Your army, taking my place on the front lines, under Your instruction. I want to know for myself, what You would ask of me.

I put behind me my dependence on others. My time of being fed with milk is over! I want to learn for myself how to be led and fed by You. Help me to be able to receive the solid food You give me. Help me to pay great attention to the signs You put before me, and teach me how to interpret them. Grant unto me the courage I need to take any actions You call me to take.

I ask You to put training tools in my hands, and discipline in my soul. Increase my faith and trust in You that You will be faithful to guide me as I obediently walk in step with You. I pray this in the mighty name of my Savior, Jesus Christ. Amen.

For the word of God *is* living and powerful, and sharper than any two-edged sword, piercing even to the division of soul and spirit, and of joints and marrow, and is a discerner of the thoughts and intents of the heart.

Hebrews 4:12

The Ancient Path

Connect the Dots:

_____

_____

_____

_____

_____

_____

_____

_____

_____

_____

_____

_____

_____

_____

_____

_____

4. THE HARRIED TRAVELER

Be still, and know that I *am* God

...

Psalm 46:10a

For thus says the Lord GOD, the
Holy One of Israel: "In returning
and rest you shall be saved;
In quietness and confidence shall
be your strength."

Isaiah 30:15

```
┌─────────────────────────────────────────┐
│                                           │
│          Strategy to Implement            │
│                                           │
│   Spend time at His feet. Divine guidance │
│   flows out of an intimate relationship   │
│             with Him.                     │
│                                           │
└─────────────────────────────────────────┘
```

Strategy to Implement

Spend time at His feet. Divine guidance flows out of an intimate relationship with Him.

"No time, no time!" the harried traveler gasped as she hurried out the door, frantically grabbing the items needed for the day and stuffing them into her bag. She was unaware, however, that what she needed most—the most important thing for her journey—was already left behind. The map and the address of her destination also sat on the counter, forgotten. But she was not concerned, because her agenda, the list of all the things she *needed to do*, was firmly grasped in hand.

Off she went to start her journey. Despite many a misdirection, wrong turn, and repeated circling of the same block, she still determinedly checked off many of the items on her list. This pleased her, for she knew she was doing it for the Lord.

The harried traveler was so focused on completing her list that she did not even notice the blood dripping from the open wounds in her head and heart; damage inflicted upon her by the obstacles set in her path. The blood soon covered her eyes and distorted her vision, but she did not even notice, as she stayed focused on doing the many good things, even great things, etched on her list.

The Ancient Path

After arriving too many times only to find it was the wrong address, or she had no key, weariness set in. Disheveled, discouraged, and heavy-hearted, she headed home to continue doing all the things she needed to do, and to take care of those who needed her care. With the dirt still smudged on her cheek from her travels, she fell into her bed to bear another sleepless night, uncaptured thoughts keeping her mind as restless as her body.

"No time, no time …" she again cried as she raced out the door, the sun still barely making itself known … and the blood … still oozing out of the wounds in her mind and soul.

✳   ✳   ✳   ✳   ✳

"There. All gone," He said, wiping her forehead. "It was just a little dirt thrown at you. It is not good to let it build up. Now, let Me see your map and the list again, My dear. Ah yes, that is the way; that is the direction you will travel today. And don't forget to take that second turn to the right at this point … it's a little tricky, and easily missed!" As she lay at His feet, His instruction continued in its steadfast tone—unwavering, calming—quieting to her soul.

"But this thing here, that one, and this one too … that is not supposed to be on your list. I have sent the others to take care of those things.

47

"I will open this door today, and that one will open next week. You'll have plenty of time to prepare. And don't forget to take the key though, or you won't be able to get in when it is time. Here it is, I'll tuck it into your bag with the rest of the things I have given to you for your journey.

"And this fight here … let Me …. there. It is crossed off."

"But Lord, that is an important fight! How can I not stand with them? Help them?"

"Yes, My love, it is a good fight, a worthy fight, but it is not *your* fight."

"O, I see. Help keep me focused on the path I am to travel."

"I will. And don't worry, I am sending a Helper with you. And when you get to this obstacle, remember what I have taught you. It will take some effort, but you can do it. Keep pressing in. You are well trained. And to defeat this one here …" He continued, whispering the secret into her ear.

"Ah yes, that is brilliant, Lord! As always! But what about that obstacle there? It is a HUGE one! How do I get by that one?"

"That one is for another day. Do not concern yourself with it just yet. You will know exactly when you need to know. And by the time you face it, you will be ready.

"And now, My little one, it is time for you to go. I bless you with safety and swift feet for your journey," He said, kissing her cheek. "But before you go, let me check your wound. Yes, the salve is working. It is healing nicely, and these bandages will keep it clean until it scars over."

And the peaceful traveler, focused, well prepared, and knowing where she needed to go for that day, set out on the path, a skip in her step and a song in her heart, fully trusting that all would be well.

And it was.

* * * * *

Let's pray.

Oh Lord …

I see myself in the harried traveler, and I don't like it! For all those times I forgot the most important thing—You—I am so sorry. Please forgive me. I repent for every time I have made a decision and left You out of it. I can be so single-focused on all of the things *I need to do* for the day, that I do not give You time to set Your agenda for my day. Too many times I have dictated my own path for my life, instead of allowing You to direct me steps, leading me on Your path, in Your wisdom. You open my eyes to see things as they really are, out from under the deception of the world. Your agenda will keep me in peace; Your agenda will keep me in joy, yet I often neglect it, instead choosing to put my agenda in the forefront. Lord, I want that to change. You are the One who puts a skip in my step and a song in my heart. Thank you. I now lay down my own agenda and pick up Yours.

The Ancient Path

Deepen my trust in You and in Your ways. Strengthen my self-discipline. Help me to capture my thoughts. Wash me; cleanse my mind each day. I want to be the peaceful traveler, the one who puts You first; the one who lays at Your feet; the one who listens to Your instructions and directives instead of charging full force ahead with their own. You give me direction. You train and equip me. You prepare me for the obstacles ahead of me. You give me all I need for my journey. You bandage my wounds. You take care of me. Help me to remember this—treasure this—and lay at Your feet every day and always. I love You with all my heart.

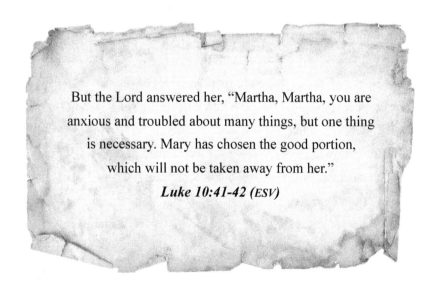

But the Lord answered her, "Martha, Martha, you are anxious and troubled about many things, but one thing is necessary. Mary has chosen the good portion, which will not be taken away from her."
Luke 10:41-42 (ESV)

Connect the Dots:

Mary or Martha? ...

_____

_____

_____

_____

_____

_____

_____

_____

_____

_____

_____

_____

_____

PART TWO

STORIES FROM MY QUEST

Show me Your ways, O LORD;
Teach me Your paths.
Lead me in Your truth and teach me,
For You *are* the God of my salvation;
On You I wait all the day.

Psalm 25:4-5

5. Seeds of Inspiration

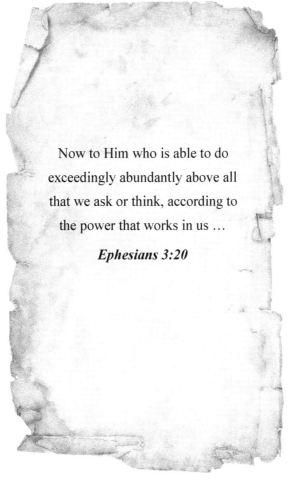

Now to Him who is able to do
exceedingly abundantly above all
that we ask or think, according to
the power that works in us ...

Ephesians 3:20

Strategy to Implement

Allow the seeds of inspiration God plants to come to their full fruit—often growing much bigger than you first think.

I woke up understanding the entire concept—seeing the big picture. Once I let it settle in, I realized *what* I was seeing. It was to be a children's book. I let my mind wander, creating the specific scenarios that would allow children and their caregivers to explore the concept God had given me. It was to be about how being led by our feelings, and subsequently always receiving what we think we want, can be disastrous. One particular situation I *knew* had to be included: the child wanting unhealthy food for breakfast. I instantly realized why. The title of this book was to be *Candy for Breakfast*.

That very day I wrote the manuscript, printed a copy, and filed it in the back of the binder I was currently using for a writing project. I was extremely thrilled with being given a children's book to write for the Lord; it was the fulfillment of a childhood dream. When I was 19, I had created and illustrated an entire line of characters, written a script, and even sewed a prototype doll. The subsequent launch of a line of characters with the same name produced as an advertisement for a film company consequently killed that dream. Now here it was again—restored to me by the Lord, and not only one book; it was to be a series. And at the end of each book would be a balloon to identify it as a part of the whole. I now just needed to know what color it would be …

The manuscript sat in the back of the binder, almost forgotten, until one day, while I was intently headed in one direction, the Lord abruptly spun me around (metaphorically) with His words, "Candy For Breakfast." I immediately put down the task at hand, and began work on the book. To my complete joy, it was brought to completion as a paper copy in my hand only a few months later. The icing on the cake came when my friend told me it was her grandson's favorite book. He had asked her to read it again and again, and now, at two-and-a-bit years old, had it memorized. What an honor God had given me!

This was not the only time I had received divine inspiration to create for the Lord. Let me share with you another story.

Being as busy as I was, taking shortcuts when the opportunity presented itself seemed prudent. Yet here I was, passing up the opportunity to do this very thing. We were at a Cleansing Stream Ministry meeting, deciding on who would teach which lessons this year. I had already taught two different ones, so logically, I could have quickly snapped up one of those, lightening my workload. But instead, I was hesitant to do so. As I held back, (or was held back) three of the topics were claimed—including both of the ones I had previously taught. Of the two remaining choices, the lesson on *Walking in the Spirit*, was tugging on my own spirit.

The Ancient Path

Within several days, I began to sense that instead of teaching theologically about this concept, I was to simply tell my stories of what following the Lord has looked like in my life. Confirmation came in the form of being awakened at 2:40 a.m. with an inspiration of a specific story to share. Flipping my light on, I jotted a quick note. But it didn't stop there. Anyone looking at my bedroom window from the darkness of the outside world would see my light flash on and off for the next two hours as idea after idea was downloaded. Then a structure of how to set it up with specific strategies these stories would illustrate began formulating in my brain. At this point, realization struck me like a hammer: "Lord, this is more than a twenty minute speech for a Cleansing Stream lesson! Ohhhhhh!!!! This is a book, isn't it!"

Though this leading of the Lord seemed quite strong to me, one question remained in my heart: "Lord, would people want to read just my little stories? Is this really what You want me to do?" Within a few days, a book I had ordered, strongly recommended to me by a friend, had arrived: Blake Healey's *The Veil*.[3] He had first drafted a book teaching about his gift of seeing in the spirit from a theological perspective. In the end, he simply told his story as *his story*. It was fascinating. I could not put it down. *Ok, Lord, You know best. People do want to hear our stories.* There is much to learn through sharing our journeys, one with another.

What about the seeds of inspiration the Lord has put within you? Are they being brought to fruition, or are they lying dormant somewhere deep in your spirit, forgotten? Ask the Lord if those hopes, dreams, and childhood aspirations, long neglected, need to be rekindled. Maybe it is time for His seeds of inspiration to bloom. Ask the Lord to show you the signs of when and how to move forward with all He has placed within you! Let's pray.

O Lord,

You are the majestic God who creates, making something out of nothing. You, who put the stars in the sky, have plans for me far above my wildest imaginings. I ask You to open my mind to all the possibilities You have placed within my spirit. Asleep and awake, fill my soul with God-inspired dreams, hopes, and desires. Please water the seeds You have already planted; grow them, and in Your timing and through the power of Holy Spirit, bring these seeds of inspiration to fruition. Let me birth everything You have designed for my life, according to Your will.

I ask You to develop in me the perseverance and character I need to carry these dreams in a way that is pleasing to You. Mold me, form me in the likeness of my Lord. I ask for the strength to be obedient and follow through on Your plans for me, no matter what it takes, no matter what it costs. I call forth the knowledge, wisdom, finances, relationships, energy, grace, and courage I need to birth everything You have set for my path.

The Ancient Path

Help me be patient in Your timing, not trying to figure it out for myself or bring it about on my own, but always sensitive to Your guiding Spirit. I pray this in the Holy name of Jesus.

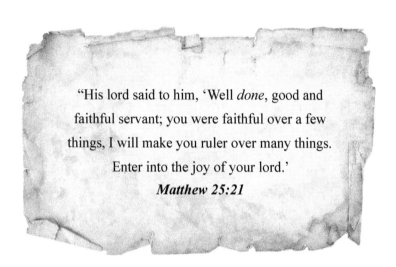

"His lord said to him, 'Well *done*, good and faithful servant; you were faithful over a few things, I will make you ruler over many things. Enter into the joy of your lord.'
Matthew 25:21

The Ancient Path

Connect the Dots:

_____

_____

_____

_____

_____

_____

_____

_____

_____

_____

_____

_____

_____

_____

_____

_____

_____

6. Surrendering our Prayer Agenda

If then you were raised with
Christ, seek those things which
are above, where Christ is,
sitting at the right hand of God.
Set your mind on things above,
not on things on the earth. For
you died, and your life is
hidden with Christ in God.

Colossians 3:1-3

Strategy to Implement

Put down your prayer agenda and listen to what the Lord would have you pray.

When the issues with a public institution threatened to become insurmountable, my friend asked me to meet with her on the building grounds to pray. The legal implications seemed to be swaying away from the side of justice for her and the future safety of all those involved. I am fairly certain she had a specific agenda she had wanted to address, but we agreed to put down our own agendas and listen to what the Lord would say—what He would have us pray. That was the only directive He had given me as I had prayed into the situation before meeting with her: walk around the entire facility, just listening. It didn't come to me as a picture or in words, but rather just a strong *knowing* that that was what we were to do.

Walking the entire lengthy perimeter in silence, our hearts were tuned in to the voice of the Lord. As we started the second loop, I asked her what she had heard the Lord saying. As we slowly retraced our steps, she began indicating many things in the natural the Lord had used as signs to her, drawing parallels to her situation.

The Ancient Path

The crumbling sidewalk, broken pipes, and chipping paint became symbolic messages to her, softly speaking to her heart. He had unfolded plans and made promises to her as we had walked, encouraging her that despite her seemingly dire present circumstances, her future was indeed bright.

As we began our third round, we began to pray from what I believe was Heaven's perspective—from the Father's heart. My friend, who had survived so many hardships in the course of her life and was now embroiled in this new battle, was able to release forgiveness over those who had wronged her—*were still wronging her.* She prayed healing, blessing, and salvation over their lives, asking the Lord to draw them into Himself. She surrendered the outcome of the legal battle into the Lord's hands, allowing herself to fully trust Him, even if it did not conclude in the manner she desired.

Though many factors of her life had been and would continue to negatively impact her to a large extent due to this situation, she was still able to set her mind on things above, and pray from that heavenly perspective. She could have become angry, seeking vengeance, or perhaps even bitter toward God, as she already had had to endure so much more tribulation in her life than many. And here she was again, fighting for her life and livelihood. Yet she was able to release the fear and lies of the enemy that would have had her grasp onto the earthly agenda and fight the battle in an entirely different manner, and most certainly not trust the Lord with the results, nor with *His plan* for her life.

My friend is one of the strongest women I have had the honor of being friends with, a warrior in her own right, yet what I witnessed the Father doing in her life as we prayed that day still brings tears to my eyes and amazement to my spirit. I believe it was a transformational moment for both of us, allowing us to grow in the depth of our understanding of what it means to let go of our own prayer agendas—our perceived needs, wants, and desires—and grab on with both hands to the things from above, seeing things from His perspective. Our trust in the ways of God grew exponentially that day, making our lives truly of those ones hidden with Christ in God.

Text update - December 2018

I am fully healed now. Asthma free since August. That tribulation taught me to allow God to fight my battle and when I learned that, the healing and miracles came. And now I have pearls of wisdom to pass to others from it; not scars and pain, but beautiful, glorious pearls. I see life so differently from walking through it. Your healing and trials were integral, as you passed them on to me to guide me through mine. The pain always heals someone else. I became strong because God led you to teach me to be a warrior. Thank you for walking beside me.

The Ancient Path

For I have not spoken on My own *authority*;
but the Father who sent Me gave Me a command,
what I should say and what I should speak. And
know that His command is everlasting life.
Therefore, whatever I speak, just as the Father
has told Me, so I speak."
John 12:49-50

Let's pray.

Thank you, Lord, for unfolding Your plans and promises to me and to those around me as I learn to listen to Your voice. Train me to hear You more clearly, so I can always pray from the heart of the Father. Help me to recognize when I am praying from my own limited perspective, focusing on my own understandings of the situation, desires, wants, and needs, instead of asking You how to pray and for Your desired outcomes. Help me to surrender the results of each negative situation in which I am involved; they are always up to You. You are in control, and You know what needs to happen in each situation. I ask You to deepen my understanding of the heavenly perspective, as through our prayers we partner with You to bring Heaven to Earth.

The Ancient Path

Help me to release forgiveness to any I still hold hostage in my heart. Help me to pray healing, blessing, and salvation over those You bring across my path—even those who have hurt me. In any areas where I am angry, seek vengeance, or have allowed bitterness to take root, I turn from that now. Help me change my thinking and my actions.

Lord, I want to fight my battles Your way, not mine, with You by my side. Make mine a life hidden in Christ. I pray this in the holy name of Jesus Christ.

Connect the Dots:

_____

_____

_____

_____

_____

_____

_____

_____

The Ancient Path

_____

_____

_____

_____

_____

_____

_____

_____

_____

_____

_____

_____

_____

_____

_____

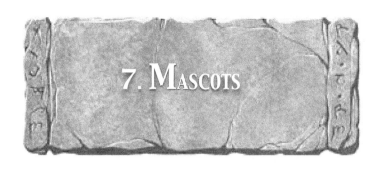

7. MASCOTS

So he answered, "Do not fear, for
those who *are* with us *are* more
than those who *are* with them."
And Elisha prayed, and said,
"LORD, I pray, open his eyes that
he may see." Then the LORD
opened the eyes of the young man,
and he saw. And behold, the
mountain *was* full of horses and
chariots of fire all around Elisha.

2 Kings 6:16-17

Strategy to Implement

Trust that what you are seeing or physically sensing is from the Lord, and that there is a purpose behind it. He is big enough to make Himself heard if you are listening, and will confirm as you ask it of Him.

Pretend you are on a tropical island, laying on a beach overlooking the water. See in your mind each sparkling wave hit the shore, leaving a trail of debris from the water in its wake. See the many colored sails of the boats dot the horizon. It is in this manner I normally *see* things in the spirit—only I don't manufacture the pictures, *thinking them up;* they just appear, usually more vivid than in my imagination, and they change without warning, one image jumping to another, seemingly random but always connected, with a volume of meaning contained within the leap.

One such example occurred during a prayer session when the image of a trap door came into my mind. Not sure as to what it meant, I continued to pray. Suddenly, I saw a paper-doll-like figure spinning cartwheels—right into the open trap door, which then slammed shut. I instinctively knew the paper-doll represented the one for whom I was praying. God's intent in giving me the picture was clear; it immediately gave us the questions we needed to ask to direct our prayer: *What was the trap? How did she come to be in it?* and most importantly, *How does she get out?!*

The Lord allows us to see the happenings of the spiritual realm for a purpose—be it for such things as to dispel fear as in 2 Kings 6, or to incite a response from us. Our task is to ask the questions and follow the trail, trusting that what we are seeing is real. As I began to see more and more things in the spirit and questioned as to whether I was "just making it all up," I continually asked for specific confirmation—God willingly obliged. This increased my confidence in that what I was seeing was from the Lord, and if it wasn't, He would eventually bring it to my attention that I had missed the mark.

And as usual, the confirmations came in surprising form. One day at church service, for example, I asked the Lord to show me what was happening in the spiritual realm. Immediately I saw in the spirit four *animal mascot-type* characters enter the sanctuary and line up along the top of the side wall, facing the congregation. They began to "pick teams," pointing to specific people in the crowd, who would line up behind them willingly, whether they wanted to or not, believing they needed to do so—did not have a choice as to which team they aligned. This process stirred up an uneasiness within my spirit because I sensed some of these "teams" were *not* on the side of the Lord. I entered into intercession, praying in my spirit language and asking the Lord what I should do with this information—what was the purpose behind me seeing it. My prayer soon transformed into an urgent, repeated cry: "Let them allow themselves to be chosen by the right one!"

Directly after I prayed, a woman I knew to be prophetically gifted stood up, asked for the microphone, and announced to the congregation that, "There are no try-outs. You can all make the team because of His goodness." Her message accomplished two things: it confirmed beyond a shadow of a doubt that what I had seen was accurate, and that the purpose of the revelation was indeed to draw me into intercession. The knowledge itself was now in the hands of each individual for them to respond as they chose. I wonder if I would still have witnessed this bizarre scene had I not asked.

But *seeing* is not the only manner in which God reveals Himself; our other senses can be involved. I have a friend who has heard both swords clashing as the spiritual battle is fought all around her and the footsteps of the troops marching above her. I have not heard to that depth at this point, but have experienced that middle-of-the-night door slamming and doorbell ringing with no one at my door. Once I heard a loud cracking of wood, which I believed was a spiritual dam breaking—later confirmed by the prophetic words of another.

The first few times I *felt* the wind of Holy Spirit, I reacted as most probably would—I checked for ceiling fans and air conditioning vents. Sometimes they were there, stirring up the air as they spun overhead; other times, not a one. Once during a ministry session in my home, I felt a gust of wind, brief, but so strong I had thought for sure I had left a window open. However, since we were in the basement with windows rarely if ever opened, and it had happened at such a strategic time, my suspicions grew that it was indeed, the person of Holy Spirit making His presence known. I had asked the others with me if they had noticed it, but they had not felt a thing. I didn't understand how they could not have felt it if it had actually happened—was it therefore my own overzealousness?

The next incident of the same variety was upgraded from a gust of wind to a blast of one. I was praying with some women in a teepee on some land specifically dedicated to the purposes of the Lord. As I was praying for the owner, a blast of wind came down through the smoke hole and exploded directly upon us, *and then went back up and out* though the hole! It was like something out of a cartoon. It left me flabbergasted. I looked around incredulously, but again, no one else seemed to have noticed it. And again I reasoned, maybe it was all a figment of my own imagination. Yet, the occurrence kept replaying in my mind. Though it was not a rational event, the logical part of me knew I couldn't have concocted something so extraordinary while in the midst of intense prayer.

When I felt that same sensation in my bed one morning, softer this time, a gentle breeze flowing over my hands, my mouth, I tested it. Repeatedly, I put my hands under the covers to see if I still felt it, or if it was perhaps a draft coming in from under my door, or maybe the air was beginning to circulate through the overhead vent. Over and over I hid my hands, yet still felt the gentle touch of what I now know was Holy Spirit. Today, when I feel His presence, that soft breeze blowing on my face, or that fresh coolness that often surrounds my hands as I write, I smile, and welcome Him. I also immediately recognize the change in atmosphere accompanying Him. The air holds a freshness you can actually smell, like winter air on a cold, crisp day, or the misty coolness one would experience as they stand by a waterfall.

Sometimes I feel that same coldness radiating off a person as Holy Spirit covers them. As I laid my hands on a friend to pray before she spoke at a function, my response was, "What? Have you been hanging out in a walk-in freezer all day?" Though her skin itself wasn't cold, she had that much coldness emanating from her.

Soon after that, while sitting on a couch next to the youth pastor of my church during another event, I literally had to get up and move away from her so I wouldn't start physically shivering. Usually when three are squished tightly together on a couch, heat is the problem, not the opposite. To best understand this, go to your freezer and pull out an item which is frozen solid—like a package of meat. Hold it about a quarter-inch from your face. That is what I feel. And to me, it is the most peaceful, sweet sensation ever. I trust that it is real, and that it is from the Lord. I then whisper, "Hello, Holy Spirit. You are most welcome here. What are You going to teach me today? …"

The Ancient Path

Let's pray and ask the Lord to help you see, feel, smell, taste, and hear more of what He has for you.

Dear heavenly Father,

You mystify me. The length, breadth, and depth of You is unfathomable. Draw me in, closer and closer to Your precious presence. Open my eyes that I might see and know more of You. Open my ears that I might hear and understand more of Your ways, Lord. God, please open all of my senses that I may be ever aware of Your presence forever all around me. Show me where You are. Show me what You are doing. Show me how I can partner with You as You bring Heaven to Earth. Take the blinders off my eyes that have kept me out of the fullness of Your glory. I bind up every shred of doubt that attempts to silence me or make me waver.

As You open my eyes and enlighten my understanding, help me follow Your leading tighter and tighter, on more and more intricate pathways. Grow my trust, Lord, by confirming all You are showing me time and time again, until I walk in confidence that You are continually by my side, never leaving nor forsaking me. Show me how there are so many more with us than with them. Help me become more in tune with the spiritual atmosphere, immediately recognizing Your presence, Your ways, Your leading, Your voice. Teach me how to strengthen myself in You, Lord. Send Your mighty rushing wind to continually fill me. Open my eyes to Your fire, Lord. Show me Your fire. In Jesus' name. Amen.

The Ancient Path

And suddenly there came a sound from heaven,
as of a rushing mighty wind, and it filled the whole
house where they were sitting.
Then there appeared to them divided tongues,
as of fire, and *one* sat upon each of them.
And they were all filled with the Holy Spirit
and began to speak with other tongues,
as the Spirit gave them utterance.
Acts 2:2-4

But your eyes shall see your teachers.
Your ears shall hear a word behind you, saying,
"This *is* the way, walk in it,"
Whenever you turn to the right hand
Or whenever you turn to the left.
Isaiah 30:20b-21

The Ancient Path

Connect the Dots:

_____

_____

_____

_____

_____

_____

_____

_____

_____

_____

_____

_____

_____

_____

_____

_____

8. NOTES, TEARS, & LETTERS

O LORD, You have searched me and known *me*. You know my sitting down and my rising up; You understand my thought afar off. You comprehend my path and my lying down, And are acquainted with all my ways. For *there is* not a word on my tongue, *But* behold, O LORD, You know it altogether. You have hedged me behind and before, And laid Your hand upon me.

Psalm 139:1-5

Strategy to Implement

The Lord wants His people to come to an awareness that He **knows** them, really knows them. Be the messenger.
(Be aware of _your_ feelings—they might not be _yours_ at all.)

"Give her a teddy bear."

"Umm…. excuse me?"

"Give her a teddy bear."

Since I couldn't pull a teddy bear out of my back pocket, I did the next best thing. I started the note I was to write to the unknown young lady with … "The Lord wants to give you a teddy bear." I can't remember what else was in the note, but seeing her outburst of tears as she connected with its contents reassured me she had received the Lord's gift to her. More importantly, the Lord had shown her that He knows her, is thinking about her, and His heart toward her is good. This is God's message to His people—and He wants to use you to be this messenger of reconciliation, bringing their hearts back to the heart of the Father.

When God wants to capture my attention so I will connect with someone in such a manner, He simply _highlights_ them to me. By this I do not mean I see a ray of light come down from Heaven to surround them, (although I have heard of this happening), but I simply *notice* them again and again. They seem to be in my sightline everywhere I look. From there, I can ask God what I am to do. Sometimes it means they are *in my tribe* and I am meant to run with them—these ones have become some of my dearest friends. Other times it means I am to pray with them or prophesy over them, take them up or stand with them at an altar call, or even send them to the prophetic ministry we have at our church.

In this method, the Lord has asked me to write letters to encourage His children: some to realign, some to step out of the shadows into ministry, some to start on a journey of healing or training. For one reluctant speaker meant to share her story, the letter knocked down the enemy's accusation against her identity: *Who was she that people would want to hear from her? What did she have to offer?* The specific directives of the Lord written in black and white and handed to her personally gave her the reassurance that yes, the Lord had indeed called her to this path, and that He *knew* her, exactly as she was, and had *chosen* her to be on His team—she was of great value to Him. The response from one other such letter was the admittance of the recipient's recent complaint: "God, it would be so much easier if You could just write me a letter!" He did. It is so fun to be the hands and feet of the Lord Almighty!

I recently encountered a woman to whom I had given such a letter several years ago. She still carries it in her wallet. She said she had shown it to everyone in her life; it marks the day *everything changed*. God is so amazing. He knows. He just *knows*.

And God, in all His creative glory, is not limited on how He captures our attention to call us to messenger duty. As I worshipped during one service, I suddenly felt a strong sense of deep, deep sadness sweep over me. I began weeping, crying out to God, and heavily interceding in my prayer language. Nothing had changed; I had not been discouraged in any manner when I had entered the building, but now I could not contain these feelings within me. Realization dawned. God was showing me something. Further prayer revealed these emotions had set in when the couple in front of me had sat down. I finally made the connection, and now I understood.

Knowing someone is hurting is one thing. You can effectively pray for them and encourage them. But when you experience the actual emotions coursing through the veins of another, feeling what they are feeling, it gives you a heart of compassion to pray for them on a new level. The urgency and fervency of prayer heightens in your spirit. You *need* to pray for them. And you understand more clearly *how* to pray for them.

My theory was confirmed after the message was given, when this couple sat in their chairs, with tears streaming down each of their faces. They seemed to want to respond to the altar call but were reluctant—almost unable—to do so. Understanding their distress and sensing the couple would appreciate another couple praying with them, I asked my house-church leaders to give them the much needed ministry. God had indeed sent this couple from another church here, this day, to receive exactly what they had needed. Most importantly, the Lord was showing them that He knows them, knows their hearts, and knows their situation; He has not forsaken or abandoned them, but is there in their time of brokenness.

We, as His children, His sons and daughters, need to be willing to put aside our fear, our pride—anything holding us back from being His messengers—and be His hands ... be His feet ... be His love to His people. Let's pray.

Dear heavenly Father,
You created the heavens, the earth, and everything in it. You created me—every fiber of my being—physical, spiritual, mental, and emotional. And You know me. You know every breath I take—every breath I *will take*. You know my heart, my desires, my weaknesses, every part of my life. And You care about every one of those parts, every one of those areas, every bit of me. Lord, it is such an honor that You know me and You choose to have such an intimate relationship with me. The level of intimacy I can have with You is truly up to me—and that is astounding!

Lord, please forgive me for not seeking You with every ounce of my heart and soul every moment that I have been drawing the breaths You have given me. I long to increase my intimacy with You more and more, with each day You give me. And Lord, I desire that those around me, those You bring onto my path, will also hunger after You and come to a deep revelation that You know them and love them. Give me Your heart of compassion for others. Please allow me to be a messenger for You, telling them of Your deep love for them.

I repent of allowing fear and pride to stop me from doing all You have asked of me in building Your Kingdom and bringing Your lost ones to You. I bind fear and pride up and cast them to Your feet. I will not allow them to hold me back for even a moment longer.

Please show me, teach me, train me to be Your messenger, in whatever capacity You have planned. I lay my life before You as an empty vessel, pleased and honored that You have chosen me for Your good works. Open my ears, open my eyes that I may be ever aware of when You are showing me something, someone to whom I am to deliver Your words of love, hope, and encouragement. Let me be bold in my faith. Fill me with Your Spirit of courage. Deepen my understanding of how and when You are speaking to me and asking me to be Your hands and feet. I ask that You bestow unto me all I need to be Your hands and feet in every situation into which You lead me. Open my understanding to Your endless creativity of speaking to me and showing me what others need and how I can help them. I am willing, Lord, send me. Send me. I pray this in the name of Jesus Christ of Nazareth. Amen.

Connect the Dots:

_____

_____

_____

_____

_____

_____

_____

_____

_____

_____

_____

_____

_____

9. Build My Temple

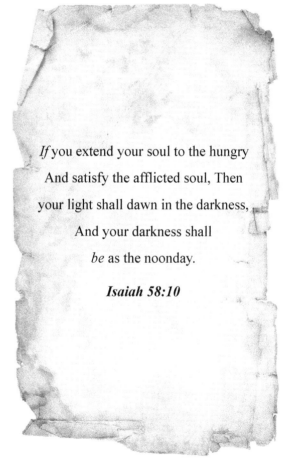

If you extend your soul to the hungry
And satisfy the afflicted soul, Then
your light shall dawn in the darkness,
And your darkness shall
be as the noonday.

Isaiah 58:10

He was sitting on the hard cement by a sign in the Tim Horton's drive-thru. I could *not* pass by without buying him a sandwich. There are times I walk past the ones on the street asking for money. On other occasions, I have been the hands of the Lord, giving food to those in need. But with this one, I *knew* I had to stop, feed him, sit by his side, and pray for him.

I ended up prophesying over him, leaving him with words of encouragement—words from God that touched his soul. The evidence of impact was announced by the tears that spilled out as those words showed him that God knew who he was and what had happened to him; those words that spoke to him of a future: one that offered hope not only to him but to others through him.

There is so much pain in the lives of others around us. Sometimes we might ponder if the little we can do for them to ease their burden in some slight manner is even worth it. It can leave us feeling discouraged, knowing the journey these ones are on will continue to be a struggle, wrought with hardships and anguish before healing and wholeness could come. Yet sometimes that is all we can give in the moment—hope. And sometimes it is enough. Sometimes it will make the difference.

I may never know what happened to this man from that day forward; I may never know if this moment in time was significant for him; but I do know it was significant for me. God used this homeless man to confirm I was hearing His voice. The exact time in my life when the Lord was instructing me time and again to *build His templ*e (this is a story in itself), He led me to feed a man on the street with the name of … *Solomon.*

It wasn't long after that time when again, I felt I was to extend my hand to one on the street. At first, I walked by as he asked for money. Once in the store, I could not let it go. Having extravagant amounts of excess funds was by no means my situation, so unless I knew for sure it was a directive from the Lord, I was not overly eager to add to my expenses, nor take the time to interact with him. I bargained. Lord, if he is still there when I leave, I'll buy him some food. Sure enough, there he was. I told him I would not give him any money but if he was hungry, I would buy him a burger. He readily agreed. Two burger meals in hand, one for each of us, we sat down on the sidewalk (me in my skirt nonetheless) for the meal I felt I was to share with him.

Jamming the food into his mouth, (it seemed it had been a while since he had last eaten) he shared with me his story. Again, my heart broke for these ones that never had a chance—the ones who had been abused since childhood, no one to love them, choosing the tough life of the streets over going home to the ones who had hurt them.

Judging by the looks we were receiving from the ones passing by, we must have been quite an interesting sight … I didn't care. What was perhaps a little uncomfortable and inconvenient to me, and maybe appeared a bit odd to others, was exactly what the Lord had asked me to do. How sad that my initial response of unwillingness had almost forfeited the honor God was giving to me of feeding this young man. And his name, meant … *crowned* … *sanctified … set apart.*

In his book, *Life is a Highway,*[4] Ian Byrd says, "Inconvenience is worship." I agree. When we set aside our selfish perceptions of inconvenience and discomfort, we will realize we are the ones receiving as we partner with the Lord to bring His Kingdom to those in need around us.

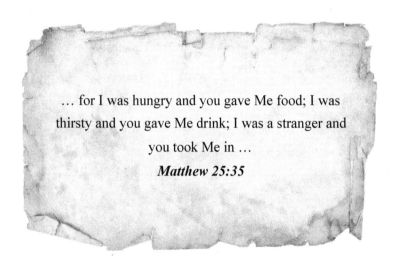

… for I was hungry and you gave Me food; I was thirsty and you gave Me drink; I was a stranger and you took Me in …
Matthew 25:35

Update: January 2019

I cancelled my work assignment this morning, unsure as to whether or not my borrowed vehicle would start on this frigid day; my province was under an extreme-cold weather warning. It did, and wanting to run it for a while, I decided my day at home called for the currently rare "Tim's run." As I pulled out of the drive-thru I saw, in exactly the same spot Solomon had once sat, another one, sitting outside underneath the sign, despite the deathly cold temperature. I gave him all the money I had on me, which amounted to the sorry total of maybe $2.00. Driving away, I burst into tears, so very grateful that I had a warm place to go. When I find myself in a place of feeling sorrowful for my apparent lack … God very quickly puts it into His perspective.

Update: March 2019

I saw the homeless one again today. He looked really rough: a black eye, scratches on his face, dark circles under his eyes, sores on his lips. He asked for money for a place to stay. He was currently sleeping in the lobby of a bank. (This next part breaks my heart to write, but I feel I am to do so.) He told me I was pretty, then asked if he could sell himself to me. Lord, please help him! What am I to do? Please bring someone onto his path that can help him!!

The Ancient Path

Please, pray with me!

Dear Lord,

Sometimes when I look at the sorrowful plight of others around me, it all seems so much bigger than me—heartbreakingly overwhelming. There is such great need and so little I can do to meet it. Please help me be Your hands and feet for the ones to whom You choose to send me. Though I can't help them all, I can make a difference in the lives of those ones You would have me do so. I want to know Your heart for these ones.

Grant unto me that heart of compassion. Show me what to do. I ask for the resources and courage to impact each of the ones to whom You are calling me. Help me make a difference. I want to build Your temple in whatever way You are asking me to do so. Let me be the prayer cry, but let me also be the feet on the ground, doing Your will in feeding the hungry, the thirsty, the afflicted, the strangers, the widows and the orphans. Let my heart break for what breaks Yours. Help me not to judge those ones who do not know You, but look upon them with love, as You do, and extend my hand, leading them to You.

Lord, I ask for protection over those ones. Keep them safe amidst a life of danger. Open their hearts and minds so they may come to You and experience the riches of Your Kingdom. I ask for restoration and redemption for them. Though I don't know any of their stories, You do. So I ask You to speak life to their spirits, minds, and bodies. You know exactly what each one needs. I ask for Your words for them that will place hope deep into their souls, so they do not give up. As I see the ones You have led me to, fill my mouth with these words they need to hear, and put bread in my hand that I may share the blessings You have given to me.

I am so thankful for everything You have done for me, and everything You have blessed me with. I am sorry for every instance in which I have taken things, and even people, for granted, rather than being grateful to the very depth of my soul. Let me be selfless in doing all You have called me to do. I ask this in the name of my Savior, Jesus Christ. Amen.

Connect the Dots:

_____

_____

_____

_____

_____

_____

The Ancient Path

10. THE SWORD

I glorified you on earth, having
accomplished the work that you gave
me to do.

John 17:4 (ESV)

We must quickly carry out the tasks
assigned us by the one who sent us.

John 9:4a (NLT)

Strategy to Implement

Follow through right to the finish that which the Lord sets before you.

"WHICH ONE, LORD?"

"It doesn't matter, just pick one!"

I had recently prophesied to a young man that the Lord was giving him a sword. Looking at me pointedly after I released that word over him, the young man had confirmed that God had given him a sword (in the spirit) during worship not two hours previous. Now here I was, at one of the scarce establishments that sell them, being the hands and feet of the Lord, who assured me it was a literal sword He wanted placed in the hands of this young man, and I was to buy him one.

The next obstacle was giving it to him. I did not know him well enough to show up at his house, sword in hand; and walking into his church with a sword, in or out of the box ... well ... seemed a bit odd, and I had visions of being arrested or causing mass hysteria. Amazingly enough, as with every situation carefully orchestrated by the Master Planner, within a week a plan was in place; we both would be traveling to the same out-of-town conference with a mutual friend.

Slightly disappointed there was no "This is it!" moment during the weekend and thinking maybe I had heard wrong, I drew his attention to the odd-shaped box at his feet as we drove home. Pulling the sword out of the box, he sat in momentary silence. The last altar call of the conference had been a commissioning of sorts, and the Lord had spiritually presented him with the *very* sword that was now in his hands. Sometimes we do not realize the depth of impact we will have for the advancement of God's Kingdom as we follow through with *all* assignments the Lord presents to us, big or small.

Some assignments, such as buying the sword, can be quick and fairly simple—one-time events. Others, such as transcribing all of the prophetic words given to me, were a little more time consuming, but no less important. It just took more perseverance and discipline. Other tasks can be extremely intense—all consuming for a season. Two overlapping prophetic words I had received led me into one such mandate from the Lord.

One of my friends believed I was going to write a book; the word *invisible* was in the title. It would encompass the issue of *identity*. Less than a month later, another ensured me I was entering into a season of identity. That was enough for me to take action. I bought a pretty black and white notebook and put it by my bedside, knowing the Lord would show me the *what* and *when*.

The Ancient Path

Months passed, with the designated journal still blank. Some would suggest to do research on a topic if you believed you were to write on it. But I know how the Lord works with me in writing. It was to be straight from Him based on my own experiences and what I had already learned—very little gleaned from third party research. Therefore, my journal sat untouched for three-and-a-half months— then I hit the proverbial wall. Personal attacks came at me from every direction, leaving me no where to go but up. As I went for prayer to my same friend, she had said, "Jocelyn, *this* is your identity stuff!" God will first take us through the lessons He wants us to share with others. I heard it once said that *it is hard to live what we preach*; God wants us, rather, to preach what we live.

The very next day for hours upon hours, the Lord took me through various steps of healing in identity-related areas, and I recorded them in my pretty black and white journal. Another wave of strange occurrences manifested over the following week, all attacking my identity. Again I buried myself away with the Lord, and He exposed more of the roots that had tangled themselves within me, corrupting my thinking and the understanding of my true identity. This phenomenon continued for about five or six weeks, until sitting in a seminar, I heard words in my head that were clearly not my thoughts: "Now write *your* workshop." And now I could. I had His blueprint in my hand. *Invisible No More—Healing Identity: A Call to Arms*[5] was born.

The Ancient Path

As the Lord's words were spoken into my spirit, it was like my life slid into heavenly alignment. *Ohhhhhh!!* It suddenly made so much sense—all of it! Everything I had been through in my personal life was being knit together with the road I had walked on my professional journey. I had formerly written manuals and presented workshops to teachers to help them improve their craft. I had just come through a many-year-long period of healing the trauma I had incurred over my lifetime, and I was involved in the healing ministries at my church. Put them all together and you have a person whose mandate is to write books and present seminars to bring healing into people's lives. I was fascinated and thrilled with God for how He had orchestrated everything in my life to bring me to this point—the point I needed to be, with all the essential experience to enable me to walk out that for which He had created me—my very destiny.

I have learned that whatever the Lord's assignment is for me, whether it be a small task in my training, or a direct part of my destiny, I am to be faithful in bringing it to fruition. It is critical that He has many in His army on whom He can trust to carry out His plan to bring Heaven to Earth. Are you one on whom He can depend? Let's pray.

Dear heavenly Father,
Just as You have knit me together in my mother's womb, You have woven my life together, forming the perfect tapestry. I thank You for

the times of training You have so carefully orchestrated in my life. I thank You for every task You've put before me to help me move into my destiny. I thank You that as I listen to Your voice and follow Your guidance, You put me on the right path.

I bind up every spirit of doubt and unbelief that tries to speak to me. I will be the unshakeable, steadfast warrior You have designed me to be. Help me be faithful in taking all the steps You call me to take—the little and the big, the easy and the challenging, the quick and the all-consuming, so I can bring glory to Your name. Develop in me the perseverance and discipline I need that will allow me to continually walk in heavenly alignment, faithfully carrying each task You have put in my hands to its full completion. Temper me, God, so I am strong and resilient, in a suitable state for all of Your purposes for me. Lord, I want to be one whom You can trust to carry out Your plans to bring Heaven to Earth. Help me be the one.

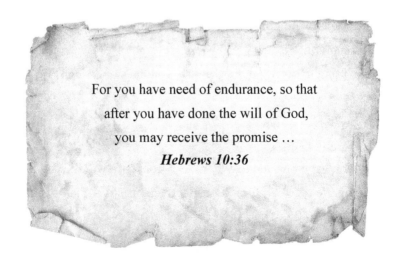

For you have need of endurance, so that
after you have done the will of God,
you may receive the promise …
Hebrews 10:36

The Ancient Path

Connect the Dots:

_____

_____

_____

_____

_____

_____

_____

_____

_____

_____

_____

_____

_____

_____

_____

11. FOWL AMMUNITION

"But now ask the beasts and they will teach you; And the birds of the air, and they will tell you: Or speak to the earth, and it will teach you; And the fish of the sea will explain to you.

Job 12:7-8

Strategy to Implement

Understand that what is happening in the spiritual realm is reflected in the natural realm; take appropriate prayer action.

"Why do I feel like I have been crapped on?" Those words gushed unchecked out of my mouth one morning while washing my face. (Sorry, just wanting to be accurate!) As my eyes met the ones looking back at me in the mirror, I responded to myself as the connection was made: "Oh, yeah. I was." You can often discern what is happening in the spiritual realm by the events transpiring in the physical realm. As I was moving forward in the plans and promises of God, and He was bringing healing to people through me, the enemy was not happy.

Just the day before, I had noticed, once again, that my vehicle was *full* of bird poop. The birds of the air were definitely telling me something, and it was not nice! This was the third time this had happened—and not just one or two messes—but *covered*. And this is not counting the two times my front door and side windows were hit with dozens of the same foul ammunition of the enemy. Considering that both the door and windows are underneath a deep overhang, I am not sure how it was even physically possible for birds to hit that target!

Calling a friend, we teamed up to pray and washed off the sludge thrown at me in the spiritual realm by the enemy. My garden hose took care of the natural side of things. My mood, needless to say, had lifted almost immediately. I may not have realized I had been "pooped on," had the enemy not once again overplayed his hand and revealed it to me through the natural realm.

This is not the only experience I have had with demonic activity displayed through excrement. I have had dreams, over and over, year after year, where I would be running around a building, desperately searching for a toilet not piled high and overflowing with human waste. However, not understanding the connection between waste (both animal and human) and demonic activity before one of my mentors had revealed it to me, I did not know I needed to be spiritually cleansed with the water of Holy Spirit and the blood of the Lamb through the reading of His Word and prayer from whatever had transpired in both the natural and spiritual realms.

Whether it had been the enemy infiltrating my mind when it was in its most vulnerable state—sleep—and literally dumping his crap, or God warning me in a dream that I needed cleansing, I am not sure. Perhaps both. Now, I pray God's word over my heart and mind as I lay down to sleep, that I may have *the Lord* teach me at night. And if I wake with the remembrance of a nasty dream, I immediately ask for revelation of what had pooped on me, so I can do my part in the renewing and washing of my mind, body, and spirit.

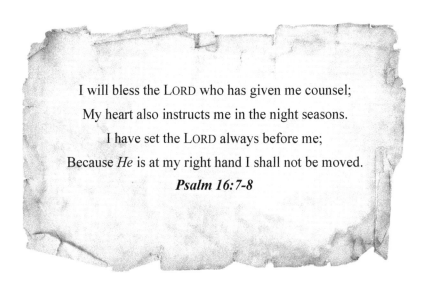

I will bless the LORD who has given me counsel;
My heart also instructs me in the night seasons.
I have set the LORD always before me;
Because *He* is at my right hand I shall not be moved.
Psalm 16:7-8

Sadly, excrement is not the only foul ammunition of the deceiver. Occasionally, usually during key ministry times, a pornographic image or sexual situation will be slipped into my dreams—the enemy's attempt to attack my purity. I am extremely careful as to what I read, watch, and wear, and to take my thoughts captive, so as to guard this area of my life, making me confident there is nothing on my part contributing to an open spiritual door.

When these dreams happen, it usually requires meeting with a trusted friend for prayer, and again washing me clean.

> Keep your heart with all diligence, For out of it *spring* the issues of life. Put away from you a deceitful mouth, And put perverse lips far from you. Let your eyes look straight ahead, And your eyelids look right before you. Ponder the path of your feet, And let all your ways be established. Do not turn to the right or the left; Remove your foot from evil.
> *Proverbs 4:23-27*

Fowl ammunition and inappropriate dreams are still not the only thing the enemy can throw at us. I had another enlightening attack while praying with a friend one day. When the Lord dropped revelation into my spirit to guide our prayer, as I started praying into it I was hit with a wave of something like *dizziness* so strong I would not have been able to stand had I not already been sitting. It had almost felt like a physical blow. My friend felt it too, saying it was like it bounced off me and hit her. My mind, ever thinking in cartoons, pictures the attack as if I had been hit by an "invisi-ray gun," or "sonic blaster," right out of a sci-fi episode.

The assault only led us to pray harder, knowing we were on the right track, or the enemy would not have come against us so strongly. Since then, I have often felt that same dizziness, though not as forceful, as I switch into intercessory prayer or when I am praying over someone. Sometimes it manifests as sudden sharp pains in my head, but I know it is just a different appearance of the same enemy tactic meant to distract or dissuade me. Thankfully, it does not work. In fact, I actually kind of like it in an odd sort of way —it tips his hand that I am onto something he does not want me to touch and makes me press in harder, knowing it is *exactly* what I need to be praying.

PROPHETIC WORD – DECEMBER 2018 (ABRIDGED)

Jocelyn, I just saw a picture and it looked like a scene out of a National Geographic where there is this deep, deep pool, and into the pool there is this rope that was suspended. It was fastened at the bottom and it went up—basically it was a waterfall it was falling in. What I saw was you climbing; and it wasn't like it was a strenuous climb; you had the strength to go hand over hand up this rope, and you were being washed continuously. Water was flowing and just washing over you. I felt like what the Lord wanted to remind you was that your mind is made new through the washing of His Word, and as you continue just to spend time and digest and meditate and ponder on His Word, there is a washing that occurs, a washing of hurts and lies of the past, washing away pain, washing away all of those things the enemy has tried to heap upon you. As you kept climbing, it was like the volume continued to increase.

—Dave Woytuik

The Ancient Path

Dear Lord,

I long to be established in Your ways, along Your paths, not the ways of this world! I thank You for revealing the events in the spiritual realm through what we can see around us in the natural. I ask for wisdom and discernment so I can clearly perceive all You are showing me and recognize what I need to ask of You, and what I need to do on my part.

I pray you wash off every bit of stink and slime the enemy has spewed on me all these years—every spot on me. Let me be clean, in Jesus' name! Any wounds which need to be exposed so they can be properly cleaned, healed, and sealed, I pray You bring to the light in Your gentle manner. I ask for the courage and strength I need to walk through the healing You are bringing me, even when it hurts. I ask for people in my life to walk with me when the road seems dark and foreboding, or even impassable. Restore hope and keep me believing that all things are possible, when You are by my side. I want to be the shining, clean vessel, fit for Your service.

I bind up any spirits of lust or perversion that are squawking at me, trying to push me off Your path. Reveal to me any spiritual doors I have left open through not taking my thoughts captive, or through my choices and behaviors. Help me to think on the pure, lovely, noble, and honorable things. Teach me to wash and renew my mind daily, that I may be transformed into Your likeness. I pray this in the name of Jesus Christ, my Lord. Amen.

The Ancient Path

Connect the Dots:

_____

_____

_____

_____

_____

_____

_____

_____

_____

_____

_____

_____

_____

_____

_____

_____

_____

12. The Typewriter

"And these words which I command you today shall be in your heart. You shall teach them diligently to your children, and shall talk of them when you sit in your house, when you walk by the way, when you lie down and when you rise up. You shall bind them as a sign on your hand, and they shall be as frontlets between your eyes. You shall write them on the doorposts of your house and on your gates."

Deuteronomy 6:6-9

Strategy to Implement

Don't miss the *remarkable* yet *obvious* signs.
But also be on the lookout for the deeper,
hidden ones.

The big, bold letters of the brandname splayed across the top of the antique typewriter caught my attention. I was collecting my belongs and heading to the door when I noticed it. I laughed and thought, *Good one, Lord!* It was *very significant* in the context of what the Lord had *just* told me at the conclusion of the prayer time at my friend's house. Some signs are so obvious it doesn't take much digging to follow their trail, nor convincing that they are indeed from Him.

This reminds me, for example, of the time I was crying out to the Lord while driving. No sooner were the words of frustration out of my mouth when I had driven up behind a car bearing the license plate: *TRSTME*. Yes, "Trust Me" had been the perfect response to my plea. And less than two weeks later, immediately after the one in the vehicle with me uttered the words, "I don't feel loved," the words on the plate that came into view were *URLVD*. "You are loved." I wonder how many times the Lord has used those two cars to reassure and encourage His people; I wonder if the drivers are aware of the stories unfolding behind them because of their obedience.

And yet again, here was another story unfolding right in front of me. During the prayer time, my friend had described her dream from the night before. In it, she remembers being in a dark space, unable to see because of the darkness. She somehow found the "door," which wasn't a door, but flaps like one would see on a cardboard box. She pushed them open and when the light came in from outside, she saw two very dead snakes (they looked like they'd been dead for a while) stuck to the flaps.

The *doors* she described reminded me of those on a cellar—the place you would go to find shelter from a storm. She and I both have spent many a year down in the cellar with the storms raging around us. "Yes," she voiced, "that was what it was!" The image of the cellar doors immediately brought to my mind Carrie Underwood's video, *Blown Away,*[6] where she walks out of the cellar and into the sunshine after the tornado had passed.

Watch that video. There is something in there for you, came the voice of the Lord. The words were not audible, more like a third-person thought … but not mine. Now, belongings in hand and passing by the typewriter, I laughed to see its brandname … *Underwood.* What are the chances? What are the odds? None. Not chance. Not even odd. It was all God.

Having watched that specific video a while ago, I was familiar with the content, and therefore not surprised I was directed to watch it again. I was, however, shocked as to my present reaction as I sat in front of the screen. The Lord was right. (Of course.) He did have something in there for me. Healing. Twenty seconds in and I was already weeping, freeze-framing, and replaying sections of it over and over. Then came printing out the lyrics, repenting, realigning, and more crying and praying as I read through them. It was an incredible experience, purging remnants of things I hadn't known were still in me. I had already left much of my past behind as I leaned into my healing these last many years, but the Lord, ever faithful, always knows which rocks to turn over and which corners to sweep.

Since that day, I have noticed I am walking in a deeper level of peace than I ever have before. Though my outward circumstances had not shifted, my soul had. And that made all the difference.

That particular sign from God was more than obvious; there are, however, times when unraveling His signs and wonders requires a little more exploratory work. Such was the time when I was painting buildings at a campground a few summers ago. Climbing up on the ladder to paint, I was suddenly overcome by a disorientating dizziness—unusual for me, even after hours of painting in the hot sun. Being back on the shaded ground brought instant relief. Determined to finish the task at hand—painting the top half of the cookhouse—I again mounted the ladder. But it was to no avail; the symptoms of heat-stroke were immediate and overwhelming ... and confusingly alleviated as my foot once again touched the ground.

The Ancient Path

Perplexed yet fascinated as I continued to ascend and descend the ladder in experimentation, the sensation finally struck me: *It is almost as if the land itself is crying out ... as if it is dying of heat-stroke.* Revelation received, I began to pray for rain from the top of the ladder in the sun, where I remained for hours, no longer in distress. Confirmation of the strange episode presented itself through a conversation initiated by the campground owner, informing me of how they were presently suffering drought-like conditions, threatening the very life of the trees.

I was awe-struck at the unconventional call to prayer God had for me that day, and it opened my eyes wide to how creative are His ways to communicate with us. It shook me awake to the fact that I needed to climb out of my box of established ways and understandings of how I heard from God, and more importantly, take Him out of the box into which I had stuffed Him. His ways of making His voice heard are unfathomable and unlimited—it was I who was limiting Him. (See "Out of the Box" in *Invisible No More, Book III.*[7])

Another fascinating mystery the Lord helped me unravel began with *tassels*. While editing the youth series, *Beyond Solstice Gates* by Kimm Reid[8] (the book series contains scriptural truth in a fictional context), I was drawn to the idea that the young heroine drew comfort from the tassels on the hem of a blanket. I was curious as to the relevance of the tassels. My curiosity was abated a short time later when I entered into the book of Numbers during my God-requested trek through the Bible.

> Then the LORD said to Moses, "Give the following instructions to the people of Israel: Throughout the generations to come you must make tassels for the hems of your clothing and attach them with a blue cord. When you see the tassels, you will remember and obey all the commands of the LORD instead of following your own desires and defiling yourselves, as you are prone to do. The tassels will help you remember that you must obey all my commands and be holy to your God. I am the LORD your God who brought you out of the land of Egypt that I might be your God. I am the LORD your God!"
>
> *Numbers 15:37-41 (NLT)*

The Ancient Path

There is indeed great comfort when the Lord's hand of protection is upon us as we obey His commands and walk in righteousness and purity. We can trust Him to guard our path as we follow His will and His ways along the ancient path.

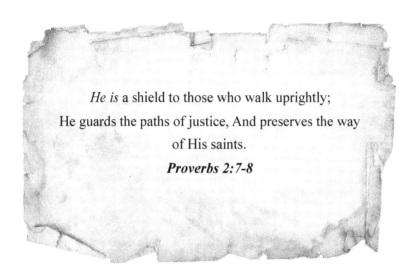

He is a shield to those who walk uprightly;
He guards the paths of justice, And preserves the way
of His saints.
Proverbs 2:7-8

When the mention of tassels again surfaced shortly thereafter at our life-group through one member's prophetic picture of a robe with tassels, I was able to speak to their significance, reading the Scripture verses the Lord had shown me. Following the emerging path, one of the group leaders presented a prayer shawl from Israel he had been gifted by a grand chief for his part in the building of 124 drums for a reconciliation ceremony. His wife, the other life-group leader, felt she was to place the *tallit* (Jewish prayer shawl) upon each of us one by one as we prayed over each other in whatever direction Holy Spirit led. As we had entered the discussion about the tassels, she had immediately thought of the *tallit* with its fringes (*tzitzit*).

The precise moment she had draped the tallit across my shoulders, I knew something was wrong—perhaps not exactly *wrong*, but oddly *different*. As I looked down, the floor was too far away. That is the only way I can describe it. When you are standing up and looking at the floor, you don't usually think about how far it is away from your line of vision, or how far away it *should* be. But when it is the *wrong distance away*, you suddenly notice it! If I did not feel the floor underneath my bare feet, I would have sworn I was standing on a small footstool. Afterward, my thoughts were, "That was bizarre," followed by the voice of the deceiver, saying, "You're making it all up!" I am grateful that this mocking voice no longer has the same impact on me.

As I later reflected on the significance of the phenomenon, I was reminded of the prophetic word a man had given me before he and his family had left for their extended mission trip to Africa. I had prayed for them after the Lord had revealed to me some of the enemy tactics at work in attempt to sabotage their journey. His parting words to me were that the Lord is going to place a cloak upon me, like the one from The Pilgrim's Progress, and that I was growing in stature. I know the reference to *stature* was in the sense of spiritual maturity, but what an incredible way the Lord chose to show me the pleasure He had taken in my growth! No one could *ever* convince me that this tassel journey was nothing more than a *really big* coincidence … Shall we pray?

Dear gracious Father,

Thank you for putting the words which You command us into our hearts. Help me teach them diligently to the children of this generation. Please help me keep them at the forefront of my mind, always in front of me, guiding my steps. Thank you for placing Your divine guidance in front of my very eyes, every way in which I turn. Help me always be aware of Your guiding hand. Please give me the strength I need to always obey Your commands and follow Your guidance so Your loving hand of protection remains firmly over me and my family. Thank you for being my shield and for guarding my path.

Lord, in those places where I still need shelter from the storm, please hide me away under the shadow of Your wing. Keep me safe and secure in Your strong tower, and lead me ever so gently into the healing I need. Please adjust and realign everything in my life not in line with Your truth and that is not pleasing to You. Purge my heart of every remnant of dust and dirt, sweeping clean every corner. Help me be courageous enough to allow You access to every door of my heart, refusing You none, so I may walk in the fullness of Your peace whether or not my circumstances are favorable.

The Ancient Path

I ask for my communication with You to open up in amazing and creative ways. Help me to recognize even the most subtle of signs. I take You out of every box into which I have tried to put You, and repent for doing so. In any areas I have shut down my communication with You through anger, pain, misplaced priorities, unforgiveness, or any other reason, known or unknown, I ask You now to forgive me and reestablish all connection between us. Open my mind and expose any areas of unforgiveness I am still harboring in my heart, keeping me from hearing Your voice and receiving Your full blessing. I pray this in the mighty name of Jesus. Amen.

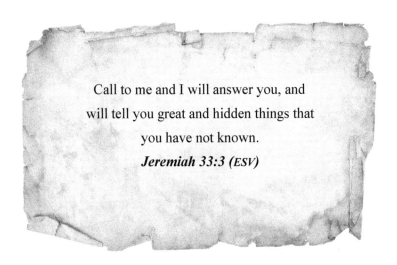

Call to me and I will answer you, and
will tell you great and hidden things that
you have not known.
Jeremiah 33:3 (ESV)

Connect the Dots:

_____

_____

_____

_____

_____

_____

_____

_____

_____

_____

_____

_____

_____

_____

_____

_____

_____

_____

13. THE GREEN BALLOON

For by Him all things were created that are in heaven and that are on earth, visible and invisible, whether thrones or dominions or principalities or powers. All things were created through Him and for Him.

Colossians 1:16

For we do not wrestle against flesh and blood, but against principalities, against powers, against the rulers of the darkness of this age, against spiritual *hosts* of wickedness in the heavenly *places*.

Ephesians 6:12

Strategies to Implement

Be patient; the Lord sometimes gives you the answer before you even know the question, rendering it impossible to know what it means at the time. Be ever vigilant; the spiritual realm is more real than the natural.

The age-old response of pinching oneself and inquiring as to if they were indeed awake was my less-than-creative albeit natural response when I first saw something in the spiritual realm with my physical eyes. Floating directly above me was a red face, much like one would expect to see if they witnessed a cartoon drawing come to life, with big, bulging eyes, straggly hair, and a small slit for a mouth; and I saw it as clearly as I see the keyboard on which I type. It stared straight at me, then rose up and disappeared into the ceiling. I wasn't scared so much as stunned.

It was then the pinching began. I never did "wake up" after that, so it confirmed I was awake all along. The Lord brought that strange face to my mind a short while later during a prayer meeting for the upcoming healing retreat. As I described it, one of the team leaders believed it to be a "watcher," assigned to transport information to the enemy. Knowing its name and existence, we were able to cancel its assignment. I don't know why this *thing* materialized to my natural eyes rather than to my spiritual ones like I saw things previously, but with that prayer came the answer to *why* the Lord had allowed me to see it. *How I saw* things did not matter so much as *how I responded* to what I saw.

Since then, I began to periodically see things in the spiritual realm with my natural eyes—but interestingly enough, to this point, only in the privacy of my bedroom, the place where I spend the majority of my time with Jesus. When I first started writing, I saw things rush at me in the night, and I may have seen them as I saw *the face*, but it was dark, and I was always awakened from a dead sleep, so I never knew for certain if I was dreaming or not. This time had been different ... entirely different. I had been wide awake. It was light in my room. It had floated above me for three or four seconds, rather than being only a brief glimpse into the unseen world. This event assuredly opened my eyes to the reality of the spiritual realm and the idea that it is more real and has as much or more impact on us than the physical objects we see around us.

The colored lights I saw floating across my ceiling one morning, like Christmas lights without the bulbs or wires, I now believe were an indication of angels being present. They were much like light being reflected off something shiny. The crisscross pattern of white lights shining above me were warnings of a trap being set. My friend told me she believed it was a web. It didn't look like a web to me, but I prayed in that direction despite my skepticism. The circumstances which unfolded that very day were confirmation enough she was right, let alone how God showed me the very same pattern replicated in my backyard soon after in the webs of a spider constructed in the grass, glistening as the sunlight hit them. The figure of a lady weeping on my bed was a call to intercession, but the meanings of several other random things I have seen still have not been revealed to me. While reading Blake Healy's *The Veil*,[3] I was reminded of the man-faced bat thing with fangs and black shadowy wings I had seen floating in the corner of my room above my bed—he had seen one much like it! His descriptions of the weird things he saw, so similar to what I had experienced, (on a much lesser level) reaffirmed the reality of what I had seen.

Journal entry - January 2017

Before going to sleep last night, I saw with my eyes, I believe, a blue ring or pipe coming out of the ceiling, or around there ... almost coming out of the heavenly dimension and going back into the heavenly dimension ... hard to explain, but it was very bright colored, bright blue, almost glowing. I think there were words on it. Almost like it came from behind a cloud, and was long, but the other side disappeared into another cloud as the other side came down ... What was this, Lord?

The Ancient Path

The blue pipe with the foreign writing on it I saw extend down from the corner of the ceiling, I found out much, much later, was some sort of heavenly communication system. God has since brought it to my remembrance and has twice asked me to implement it during times of spiritual warfare with a friend over the American political situation. I thought this was strange, even for me, until the gorilla walked through my bedroom in the early morning hours.

There … was … a … gorilla … in my bedroom. "Okay, Lord, what is *that* about?" Then I understood—guerrilla warfare. He knew I'd make the connection. I asked Him what was going on in the spiritual realm, and He showed me, with my spiritual eyes, a squadron of men surrounding me, all with bows and arrows ready to fire … and all *pointed right at me*. I was thankful He chose to use my spiritual eyes this time. Seeing the gorilla in the physical was enough. When the word *garrison* appeared in my devotion later that morning, I knew it was the Lord, confirming what I had felt and had seen. A *garrison* is a military unit, battalion, or company—exactly what I had witnessed. With that information, I was able to pray specifically against it, both for me and for another for whom He sent me to pray.

Another time, I had believed the *ogresque* creature I saw sitting at the end of my bed, back to me, was on our side of the war, even though he wore a spiked collar, when I heard in my spirit what I thought was his name—Guardian. It wasn't too much later that the true nature of the guardian was brought to me through an emailed prophetic word. It was a *guardian spirit*, brought as opposition against me, and worse yet, was sent to turn others against me, and me against them, releasing false fear and suspicion. Not fun, but good to know.

The figure I saw floating above the end of my bed, the cartoon outline of a man, like one would see on a washroom facility but with one leg all twisted, led me to pray with our healing team for those with leg injuries. The *gollum*-like hunched-old-man-creature let me know the enemy was not happy with the sword-fight warfare into which the Lord had recently been leading me (see Zoro and the Ice Man). Some of the figures from the spiritual realm that I have seen with my natural eyes I still have not yet discovered why I saw them, what they meant or were doing, nor what I was or am supposed to do with the information. Perhaps I'll never know. Maybe I don't need to know everything, but I just have to ask, and trust that the Lord will let me know everything I need to know, when I need to know it.

But the green balloon, the one I saw hover above my bed for a length of time before it disappeared into my ceiling, that one I did eventually discover beyond a shadow of a doubt its purpose. It was in answer to the question I had asked too many times before catching on. I had, in fact, seen the answer, the green balloon, long before I even knew what the question was, or that there would even be such a question. *"Green, Jocelyn. Green. The balloon is green."* (See *Seeds of Inspiration.*) Please join me in prayer.

The Ancient Path

Dear Lord of Hosts,

You have created all things in Heaven and on Earth, visible and invisible; and by Your will they exist and were created. And You reign supreme over them all. Even the principalities, powers, and rulers of darkness must bend their knee to You, now and for all eternity. You alone are worthy to receive glory and honor and power.

Lord, You see my battles, You know all my fights, and You already know how the victory is to be won. I ask for wisdom, insight, and revelation, that I may walk onto the battlefield assured of the victory in every circumstance, in Your perfect timing. Take the blinders of the enemy off my eyes that I may see and know Your truth. Expose any deception to which I have fallen victim. Anoint my eyes with eye salve, that I may see. Reveal to me the plans of the enemy, that I may release instead, Your plans. Help me remain ever vigilant, aware that the enemy is stalking the earth, looking to kill, steal, and destroy; but even more aware of Your grace, power, and mercy. Open any cages keeping me captive. The Blood of the Lamb and the finished work of the cross covers all—covers *all*. Amen.

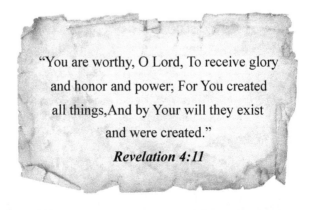

"You are worthy, O Lord, To receive glory
and honor and power; For You created
all things, And by Your will they exist
and were created."

Revelation 4:11

The Ancient Path

Connect the Dots:

_____

_____

_____

_____

_____

_____

_____

_____

_____

_____

_____

_____

_____

_____

_____

14. THE BANNER

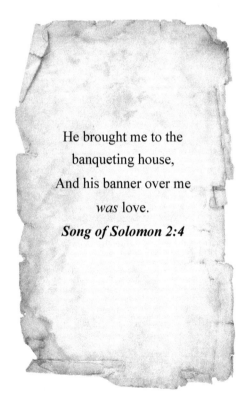

He brought me to the
banqueting house,
And his banner over me
was love.

Song of Solomon 2:4

Strategy to Implement

God is intentional. Always follow His leading, no matter how subtle.

My first thought as I felt the material drag across my hands was that I was too close to the one doing warfare with the flag. God had called me to my knees at the back of the sanctuary, face down, hands stretched out before me in surrender. But as the banner continued to rhythmically cover my hands—only my hands—time and again, I sensed intentionality.

"Lord, is she doing it *on purpose*?"

"Does it matter? I am doing it on purpose."

Wanting to respect her obedience if she indeed knew she was fulfilling God's purposes, (and avoiding any potential awkwardness) I concentrated on my conversation with the Lord and refrained from lifting my head to satiate my curiosity.

"What is it, Lord?"

"Waves and waves of My love."

Talking to her afterward, she confirmed it had been a specific directive of the Lord. Despite her hesitancy because we did not know each other, she had carried out what had been requested of her.

"What was it for you?" she had asked.

"Waves and waves of His love," I started, then out of my mouth flowed the words of other anointings and blessings that had all been contained within the touch of His banner over me—over my hands. And this all came on the heels of the Lord anointing my mouth at the altar the previous night. He had the pastor touch my mouth. (She had been concerned about the mosquito repellent on her hands!) As she touched her finger to my lips, my body went weak and I stumbled back. Knowing it was not done, I stepped forward. She faintly touched them once more and down I went again, my nervous system completely overwhelmed by the power of God.

I say *again* because in the moments prior to this anointing I had been on the floor for an extended time, weeping (and perhaps wailing)—grief I hadn't known still remained after my intensive pursuit of healing—coming up from the depths of my belly. Three of *my tribe*, who all had "inexplicably" ended up at this same camp meeting, were intensely praying over me, providing the covering I desperately needed to allow for these vestiges of trauma to be ripped from the core of my being.

The Lord was leading me through an intense purging and cleansing, a surge of Holy Spirit water knocking down and cleaning out debris from the wall of disappointment and unbelief I had constructed around my heart, built upon the back of the hidden grief.

I had been a little surprised this wall was there, as the Lord had healed me from so much pain already; yet I should have known, as many a time He has gently reminded me that healing comes in layers, each one going deeper and deeper. And this wall had to be removed prior to the anointing on my mouth and hands I know now He had carefully orchestrated to bestow upon me that weekend; otherwise, I could not have received it. Frozen hearts and walled hearts block much of His blessing.

And I had only known this wall existed when I had gone forward for prayer the first night from this same pastor. Instead of praying she had pulled back, hearing from Holy Spirit and specifically informing me I had a wall to deal with. I had spent the following afternoon stubbornly conversing with Holy Spirit (perhaps arguing a little), as to the wall's existence, and after He readily assured me she was right, as to what it was. Thankful for her obedience in being blunt with me instead of simply ignoring it and praying for me anyway, I was then able to repent for not trusting God, which had allowed the construction of the wall of disappointment and unbelief designed to rob me of my blessing, anointing, and ministry from God. This repentance enabled me to come out of alignment with the enemy's plan for my life, and come back into alignment with God's plan, opening the door for the events I have described, to transpire.

The Ancient Path

God had done an awesome work in me that weekend, both in healing and in blessing and releasing me into ministry. It was not only miraculous what had happened once I had arrived at the camp, but in *how* He had led me to be there in the first place. I had been sitting at my desk on the last day of school, and a colleague had walked in, asking if I was planning on attending the worship weekend at Springside Camp. I had briefly visited that particular camp thirty years previously, but I knew nothing of the camp since that time, and had not received any information about the event set to occur in less than two weeks.

"Leave me the details, if you would, and we'll see if the Lord gets me there!" was my response, as it did not look at all feasible to make plans to attend at that particular time. Within several days, however, I had found out my children would be away most of that weekend. The fact I was informed of their plans ahead of time was significant to me, as communication is somewhat lacking in my family at times—information is often distributed last minute, or after the fact. That in itself grabbed my attention.

"Maybe the Lord wants me to go to that worship weekend…"

Shortly thereafter, as I explored the possible option in conversation with my sister, who was at the time trying to fill her blank-slate of a summer, she excitedly hopped on board, readily supplying a travel companion and cutting the overall cost of the excursion. With those things in place, I felt it was indeed the leading of the Lord. And after my experience that weekend—it was undeniable.

I should have figured out something was up, that this weekend was to be life-changing for me, when during the first service I received a prophetic picture, word, and directive for another sitting several rows in front of me, and for the first time ever, I felt I was *not* to share it with her. In fact, I was not even allowed to pray for anyone—I was to only *receive* the whole weekend. "Okay, Lord," I had conceded, "but if I am not to share it with her, can you send someone else to tell her?" At lunch that day, my sister had said she received a word for a lady, and needed to go pray with her. I was not at all shocked as she pointed her out to me …

Interestingly enough, God also sent two more people to specifically bless and anoint *my feet* within the next couple of weeks. My *mouth*, my *hands*, then my *feet*—all within a two week or so span of time. Finally, I was given Song of Solomon 2:4 shortly thereafter as confirmation. Curious. I wonder where the Lord is taking me…

God is so good. He will speak to us, lead us and guide us into amazing treasures. And He prefers not to have to use a *sledgehammer* before we hear His voice and follow His leading. Follow those slight God nudges, no matter how subtle. You never know to what exciting path they will lead. The closer you become to the Father's heart, the more subtle the nudges He has to give; and the less it takes to "convince" you it is His voice, the quicker you can respond. It is then that you can flow together in the dance of the Father.

Let's pray.

Dear loving Father, Jehovah Nissi, my Protector,
Thank you for spreading Your banner of love over us each and every moment of our lives. Under Your banner we find Your presence and protection. In it we find Your victory. I repent for not trusting You to protect me. I ask You to forgive me for not trusting You with those tender, vulnerable places of me. Who better to trust with every aspect of my being than the One who created me—the One who created the heavens and everything in it? Draw me in closer to You, that I may trust You more—trust You with everything and everyone in my life.

Lord, I ask You to spread Your banner over me and draw out any grief, pain, disappointment, unbelief, and other debris trapped in the depths of my heart, known or unknown to me. Expose any lies to which I have fallen prey. Waters of Holy Spirit, surge through me and wash every part clean. Knock down any walls I have constructed and thaw any frozen parts of my body, soul, and spirit.

I come out of alignment with the enemy's plans for my life and step into alignment with Your plans to prosper me, not to harm me, but to give me a future and a hope. Let me hear Your still, quiet voice louder and louder, the closer I come to Your heart. Lead me into Your love, Your blessing, Your anointing. You honor me as I honor You. You celebrate me as I celebrate You. I honor You, Lord. I celebrate You. I celebrate You. In Jesus' name I pray. Amen.

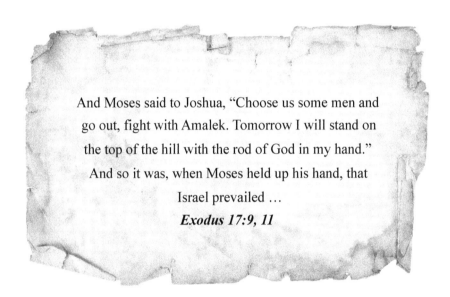

And Moses said to Joshua, "Choose us some men and go out, fight with Amalek. Tomorrow I will stand on the top of the hill with the rod of God in my hand." And so it was, when Moses held up his hand, that Israel prevailed ...

Exodus 17:9, 11

The Ancient Path

Connect the Dots:

_____

_____

_____

_____

_____

_____

_____

_____

_____

_____

_____

_____

_____

_____

_____

_____

_____

15. A Necessary Posture

Therefore humble yourselves under the
mighty hand of God, that He may exalt
you in due time, casting all your care
upon Him, for He cares for you.

1 Peter 5:6-7

Then he said to me, "Do not fear,
Daniel, for from the first day that you
set your heart to understand,
and to humble yourself before your
God, your words were heard; and I
have come because of your words.

Daniel 10:12

Strategy to Implement

**Humbling yourself before the Lord is a
rewarding posture.**

I awoke in the night to an angel standing by my bed. It was almost
one of those *Am I really seeing this, or am I dreaming* moments,
except he was still there for several seconds after I was fully
conscious. My body was still carrying the *startle effect*, which was
also a sure sign I was seeing with my natural eyes. I could not see a
face or any wings, but he was wearing a vested tunic of sorts and
carrying a white container.

I asked the Lord who he was and why he was there. Once my
heart calmed, I drifted back to sleep. I was curious as to what was in
the bucket …

The next morning, though running slightly late, the lyrics in a
worship song caught my attention. My scurrying paused, I was
drawn to my knees, face down in worship to my God. My heart still
softens with the remembrance of those few minutes. As the moment
drew to a close, still on my knees, I tilted my head and opened my
eyes. From this posture, brought into sight behind me and under the
dresser, was the elusive tie for my curtains. Though I had not

searched extensively for it, I was glad it had surfaced, and out of my mouth burst forth, "Thank you, Lord! Now if only I could find my ring too!"

My ring, normally locked away in a firebox, had inadvertently been dumped out and buried beneath the contents of my closet during the most recent purging efforts. As I had sorted my way through the mile-high stack of clothing and other various items, and my bed once again saw the light of day, I dolefully discovered the open box. One of the two rings I had kept in it was still there, along with my paper valuables. My diamond ring, however, was gone.

For weeks, on hands and knees, I had scoured every potential hiding place, but to no avail. I eventually concluded that it must have ended up in the donation bag, in some pocket or fold of clothing, on its way to be a blessing to its unexpectant recipient. With those words barely off my lips, I froze. There, perched up on the fibers of the carpet, almost like it was being presented to me, was my diamond ring.

Humbling myself before the Lord in the privacy of my prayer closet (or when that is the climate of a gathering) has always been easy for me. But the first time the Lord had called me to a posture of humility during a regular church service, I was hesitant. He had called me to kneel during worship, when no one else was doing so. It had required most of the song to have played by the time I had finished bargaining. *If they play the chorus one more time, then I'll do it... Maybe after the next verse ... People will think I'm over the top* ... In obedience, I finally had submitted. The Lord blessed me, and I felt a new level of connection with Him.

Afterward, one of the worship leaders mentioned that when she saw me go to my knees, she too, knelt down on the stage. In my focus on the Lord, I had not noticed. Her statement, however, helped me understand that when we do what the Lord asks of us, we are not the only ones impacted. In her obedience, how many other people were drawn to reverence of the Lord's majesty as she knelt in front of the congregation? Fear of the Lord needs to be restored to its rightful place over fear of man and thoughts of man. Humbling yourself before the Lord brings restoration—both internal and external. It is indeed, a rewarding posture.

We shall put our words to action, kneel before the Lord, and pray to our Majestic King.

My heavenly Father,

In the words of David, "You are clothed with majesty and girded with strength. From everlasting to everlasting, You are God. Your mercy endures forever! How lovely is Your tabernacle, Lord of hosts! Great are You, and greatly to be praised!"

I cast all my cares onto You, for You care for me. I humble myself under Your mighty hand, as You are the strength of my life. I set my heart to understand Your ways—I long to know You, O Lord! Please hear my cry! Keep my heart soft—forever clay in Your hand.

I repent of all fear of man. I turn from the selfish desires of the flesh. I no longer want to base my decisions—my obedience—on what others will think or what I want. Let me live only to please You! Instill in me the reverent fear of the Lord, my God. I bind up any pride or false humility that keeps me from deep relationship with You. I bind up any rebellion, independence, or self-reliance that keeps me from submitting to You and Your ways. Captivate my heart as I surrender it unto You. Perfect Your holiness in me, Lord. Let me be a sanctified vessel that will draw others unto You. Jesus, may You reign in my heart forever and always. I love You. Amen.

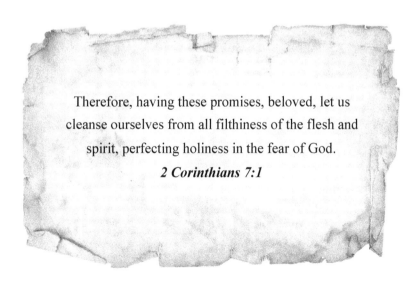

Therefore, having these promises, beloved, let us cleanse ourselves from all filthiness of the flesh and spirit, perfecting holiness in the fear of God.

2 Corinthians 7:1

Connect the Dots:

_____

_____

_____

_____

_____

_____

_____

_____

_____

_____

_____

_____

_____

_____

_____

_____

16. CHINKS IN MY ARMOR

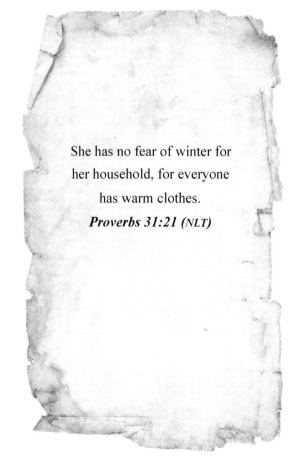

She has no fear of winter for
her household, for everyone
has warm clothes.
Proverbs 31:21 (NLT)

> # Strategy to Implement
>
> **God exposes our fears so He can heal them.**
> **He doesn't want any chinks in our armor.**

live version journal entry...

November 10, 2018

I am afraid of winter. (It is somewhat ironic I live in Canada.) I didn't even know it was a real thing of which one could be afraid. And I didn't know this fear had a hold on me until yesterday, when the familiar feeling of vulnerability came sneaking in with the cold as the temperature tanked for the first time this year. Hating the cold is one thing—but fearing it is another. As I acknowledged this sensation, it dawned on me that this uneasiness does not relent until the threat of deadly frigid temperatures has passed. God is again lighting up the dark places I still carry.

I was stepping into my warm house after plugging in the block heater to my vehicle, (we really do this in Canada) when this realization hit. *I feared the cold temperatures.* They make me feel weak and helpless. Many things can go wrong with a vehicle in winter, leaving you stranded and exposed to the elements. And the furnace—always subject to mechanical failure—is the only thing keeping my family warm on those freezing nights. The thought of anyone being alone somewhere in the cold, unable to get help, is overwhelming to me. I cannot comprehend how the settlers and pioneers of old had survived those freezing prairie winters. I admittedly would rather die than be trapped somewhere in the cold. This is not good! It sets up negative expectations—and expectations often get met.

Tears spilled as I shared my newly-exposed (but not newly-existing) fear with several people last night. And now, as I write this, the Lord is speaking to my heart, telling me it is connected to a spirit of control. I have no control over the winter, the cold, and all the potential hazards. I am utterly powerless. And I am not trusting God to keep me safe. This is *a chink in my armor.* (That was the term given in prophetic prayer last night.) But the Lord wants to heal this in me.

I know He had healing in the wings for me because of what happened next. This morning, excited to finally have a day completely focused on writing, I became sidetracked and began cleaning a book shelf. Slightly perplexed as to why I wasn't taking full advantage of the quiet house and rare uninterrupted block of time, I "randomly" pulled out one of the ten devotionals scattered throughout the shelf, curious as to what it would say for today. Though it was not the message behind the thought for the day, the words of Proverbs 31:21 were there, in black and white, as part of the text: "She has no fear of winter for her household, for everyone has warm clothes."

I would have read that Scripture several times as I had read through my Bible, but I had never *noticed* it before. And I wouldn't have ever recalled it or thought to request of Siri if any Scriptures existed about fearing the winter … as it did seem rather odd, even to me. *But there it was.* The very next day. What are the chances? None. It is God, letting me know He wants to repair the chink in my armor by healing me of my fear, doubt, and mistrust of His ability to keep me and my kids safe from not only the deathly cold, but from other dangerous circumstances. I guess I'll be sitting down with Him in the next little bit, and see where He leads me.

November 12, 2018

My family was in a car accident when I was about 6 years old. It was not serious—no one was sent to the hospital, and I don't even remember the actual feeling of impact. But it was before the seatbelt era, and it must have scared me. It planted seeds of fear that me and my family were not safe. (More on this area in *Invisible No More Book II: Personal Identity Restored*[9]) This is what the Lord brought to my mind as I repented for not trusting Him to keep me and my loved ones safe and asked Him to reveal what had opened the spiritual door to this fear.

As I prophetically pulled out the root of fear, I saw that this seed had sprouted a whole root system. Another experience connected to it was my brother's motorcycle accident; at 18 years of age he had become an amputee. It was a miracle he wasn't killed. The death of one of my eighth grade students in an ATV accident was another event that had planted fear and trauma in my heart. My first niece was stillborn. It too, was a traumatic time for my entire family. I wrote a poem in her memory, and my eyes still mist as I now type the words, almost thirty years later:

With tears in my eyes I finally said
"Good-bye" to the precious baby we love so much.
But my heart still aches for her, and my eyes still cry.

She was taken from us, taken before her
Very first breath of life. She was carried and loved
For nine months, but her life ended;
Ended as suddenly as it had begun.

Though we never saw her life, we held her.
Though we never felt her breath, she touched us.
She touched all of our lives in a very real and special way,
Leaving a painful place in our hearts
That will never heal.

We miss her, as only emptiness fills that place

Where she should have been.
But I know, deep in my heart, that she has gone
To a better place, and that one day I'll see her
And be able to say, "I love you."

But for now, my heart still aches for her,
And my eyes still cry.

Through these events, God revealed the fear was connected to a spirit of death and destruction, and I remembered the times in my life I felt like I *could have* or *should have* died. Twice I almost drowned (my older brother rescued me one of those times). I also should have been electrocuted as the mast of our sailboat hit a power-line while I was hanging on to the metal forestay. I had felt the shock but did not get hurt. My parents couldn't understand how I did not receive a much greater jolt.

The Lord then showed me how He has had His hand on me, keeping me safe. He knows the number of our days before He takes us home (Job 14:5). Once as I was crossing the street as a young teen, hood over most of my face to fight the cold, my friend reached out, sightly putting her hand in front of me. Normally, I would have just looked at her to see what was up … and kept walking. But for "some reason," this time I *instantly* froze. A car raced past, inches in front of me.

The Ancient Path

Another time, as a young driver, I was on the highway and I started nodding off. In scared reaction I called out to God, and immediately felt a jolt of electricity go through my spine, making me jolt upright and snapping me awake. There was no way I was falling asleep after that! A third incident the Lord brought to mind was when I should have been in another car accident on the highway. I actually closed my eyes and braced for the impact that should have but never came. I don't know how I wasn't hit, but I opened my eyes as my car came to rest a few feet from a steep embankment.

Yes, the Lord has had His hand on my life. And nowhere is it more evident than in the fact that I even exist. I've asked my dad, a writer in his own right, to share his experiences.

Looking back at my life from the age of 85, I recognize events where God stepped in to protect me (in some cases from consequences of my own ill-advised actions). In fact, I believe I could have died in my youth as the result of choices I had made. But God intervened. It is hard to explain it otherwise. I am unable to be precise about the age I would have been at the time of the events that come to mind. They would not have been recorded as

147

memorable historical events! But they are memorable in that I survived to record them. I cannot claim to have asked God for an intervention when these things occurred, but the events themselves suggest a supernatural hand could be the only explanation as to why at least three separate incidents did not claim my life in my childhood or in my early youth, somewhere between the ages of 5 and 13.

The first I will describe was the event I called "the straw pile incident."

As a farm boy, one of the most interesting times was threshing time. During that period of farming practice, the "threshing gang" approach was common in Southeast Saskatchewan. The "gang" of that day did not evoke a picture of drugged-up youth out for trouble, but rather a group of farmers co-operating to most efficiently get their crops off the fields and into the bins. One of the group would have been the owner of the threshing machine itself, and of a tractor with sufficient power to operate it. He had the machine, but not the manpower to haul the sheaves of ripened grain, drying out in *stooks* out in the fields, to the stationary threshing machine. Combines, of course, had not yet come into common use, and were too expensive for an individual farmer to own. So by convenience of location, several farmers got together to form the "threshing gang."

It was a most admirable example of co-operation. The neighbors, usually, of the owner of a threshing machine, joined that owner and became a "gang." They would provide the horses, wagon racks, and muscle to haul the *stooks* of grain to where the machine was set up on an individual farmer's land. The owner of the machine became the temporary employer who "hired" the local farmers, and/ or their grown sons old enough to handle a team of horses and load the racks with sheaves of grain to haul them to the machine. He would pay them for their labor at an agreed rate, meanwhile charging them a rate for the threshing that his machine would perform on their individual farms. I can recall wages for sheaf haulers of somewhere around $4 - $5 per day, while charging for threshing services a price per bushel of crop threshed—9 cents a bushel for wheat, 4 cents for oats, etc. In the end, if all went well, the owner of the machine got his crop threshed for free, and had enough left over to pay for upkeep of the machine. I remember, when I was old enough to understand those aspects, that I was proud of my dad for being the "thresher man" for a good part of my youth. I remember, as well, that he was diligent and generous with people who for whatever reason had trouble meeting their obligations. There was often a need as well for someone with a strong back and a team of horses to haul the wagon boxes of newly-threshed grain back to the yard or wherever storage bins were located. As time went on, farmers provided portable bins which could be drawn out into the fields to contain the newly-threshed crop, and in those cases the threshing machine would set up next to it.

Harvest time was a lot of work for my parents, and there was work for the kids, too. I remember, (not at all fondly), *stooking!*

The Ancient Path

That involved setting the bundles of grain cut and tied by the binder into *stooks*, little tents made of the sheaves, on their ends to keep the heads of grain off the ground in case it rained between harvest and threshing. Back-breaking, boring, striving, sweating—are descriptions of *stooking* that come to mind. After perhaps two weeks of drying and curing, the sheaves of grain were usually ready to be threshed, and that operation entailed much labor as well.

Most of that labor was in shoveling grain and helping to unload the large wagon-boxes of wheat brought in from the threshing machine into our yard, to be unloaded into granaries, where the grain was stored. It was hot, dusty, itchy work, but there was a lot of time between loads when I could watch the exciting action of seeing the sheaves of wheat go into the machine at one end, and the grain come pouring out the other, through a noisy, grinding auger. I especially loved to see the threshed straw shoot out of the blower, gradually building a steadily growing, soft pile of fresh yellow straw. Depending on the length of time the machine would stay at that spot, the straw would eventually become a great pile, some 20-25 feet high or more, some 20-30 feet in diameter, and remain there, in some cases, for years. For that reason, they would attempt to set up the machine so the resulting straw pile would not consume usable land; sometimes it would cover some of the trees that might be at the edge of the cultivated land. Over the winter, of course, some of the straw would be hauled to the farmyard to be used as bedding in the stalls of the animals. In other cases, a straw pile would be burned if it was covering usable land.

On the occasion I speak of, the threshing gang was threshing the wheat on some land my dad had temporarily rented located on the other side of a small valley cutting partially through our farm. It would have been approximately a half-mile from our farmyard. I honestly cannot recall whether I had asked permission, or taken off on my own to "go see the threshing!" But at any rate, I was there, watching the grain pour down the spout into the wagon, "helping" by playing in its coolness on a warm autumn day, and meanwhile watching the straw shoot from the blower, a golden shower slowly building an oblong pile. It was a "young" pile, about 6 or 8 feet high, perhaps …

Suddenly, there was some problem at the front of the machine. My uncle, who at that time was still the "thresher-man," shut off the belt drive from the tractor, and the machine groaned its way to a halt … some small problem had come up. Hmmmm … that straw pile looked so neat, so exciting! No straw was coming now, as the men sought to correct what had gone wrong at the front end of the machine. I HAD to climb that straw pile! I did not ask permission; I knew I would not get it. At the least, straw was itchy when it got into your collar. Like, why would you want that? But on bare feet it would feel great; my feet were as tough as leather from going barefoot all summer, over grass, gravel, or mud or stubble. So up the straw pile I worked my way; nobody had seen me climbing slowly upward, sinking deeply into the straw of the fresh pile. I just HAD to make it to the top! And slowly, slowly, I got closer and closer to the highest point. Each step had been harder, but I persevered, barely able to get my rear leg out to move to the next step. But the higher I got, the deeper I sank, and no one knew I was there. Uncle Louis was at the front end of the machine, and they were working to clear the problem. Meanwhile I had achieved my goal, the top of the pile! But no one was there to congratulate my climb of Everest!

And at the precise time I discovered I couldn't get my feet out of the straw high enough to take a first step downward, I heard the tractor start up! The machine would begin to blow more straw within a minute or two, once they had determined it was good to go. But there I was—stuck up to my waist and unable to free my feet to take a step. I began to scream, "Help! Help! I'm stuck! Help! I'm stuck!" I kept shrieking, but no one could hear, because I was at the rear of the machine, and the tractor was running, as my uncle was about to start the works of the machine. Straw would soon come shooting once more out of the blower. I heard the machine begin to clunk and clank as they tested it slowly at first to see that it was running freely, and then they would resume feeding in the sheaves. I was about to be buried in straw, because I couldn't move. I screamed again, "HELP! HELP! I'M STUCK IN THE STRAW PILE! PLEASE HELP ME!" No one could hear! The machine was running faster and faster, but no sheaves had been fed into it yet … but when it was up to full speed they'd never hear my feeble cries from the back of the machine … I was struggling, succeeding only to sink more deeply, when suddenly a team of horses with a half-loaded wagon came racing up from the field where Joe Tochor had been loading the last *stooks* of sheaves in a small arm of the field behind the machine and off to the side.

"STOP THE MACHINE! STOP THE MACHINE!" yelled Joe as his team came galloping up to where he could be heard. The machine had gotten up to speed, and some straw began to filter down, but then it slowed, and a few moments later Uncle Louis struggled up the pile, or should I say through the pile, for he sank into it, too, and asked me what I thought I was doing there. There was some laughing, but not much, for everyone realized what a narrow escape I had had. I knew, too, that I was going to "catch it" when my folks found out about it. I tried to think of an excuse, even a way to blame someone else. But surprisingly, I was not severely punished, as far as I can remember; I think my parents knew I would not be pulling another such stupid move for a long, long time!

The miracle? How was there a miracle? Well, for one thing, the small section of field where Joe had been collecting the last few *stooks* was the **only place** I could have been heard. Every other team and driver were much too far, on the other side of the machine, with the noise of the starting machine between them and my screams. There were only a few stooks left where Joe had chosen to go, and from where he had heard me screeching my lungs out. He could hear me because I was the closest to him, between him and the noisy machine. Many times I've pondered the combination of "circumstances" that made my rescue possible. It would have been a slow, choking death, and no one would have known to where I'd disappeared. Who'd have thought to look under a straw pile?

Only many years later, when I had become convinced that God cares about each one of us, did I begin to understand that I'd been the recipient of God's grace. Did I deserve it? Certainly not! I was not only in the wrong place at the wrong time, but my God was the only one who knew I was there, and knew that one day I would grow up to know Him and trust in His Blessed Son to save me from my sins—just as He arranged things so I could be saved from the straw pile and live my life even if, as it happens with many, we don't really "deserve" a second chance.

Obviously God knew I needed to live to become the daddy to the daddies and mommies of my precious grandchildren! They have a right to live their lives too, just as God thought I did! At the time I thought I'd been really lucky. But some later events suggested strongly that Someone wanted me to live out my life.

Not much later—again I did not record any dates or my age at the time—another episode in my life needed the hand of God! I seemed to have a gift for getting in trouble; some of it quite innocently, however.

The next event that defies explanation happened when I was about 10. We were innocently on our way to school, walking the 2 miles as usual. (Don't forget, "them new-fangled kilometers" weren't used *way back then*!) It had rained overnight, and the dirt road was muddy and slippery as we sloshed our bare-footed way to school. We had about a mile of our journey yet to go, when suddenly, along came a shiny red Massey-Harris "101" tractor, its engine purring smoothly as befits its streamlined design and RUBBER TIRES! (Our John Deere Model AR had steel wheels and ugly steel lugs for grip on the soil.) This was a neighbor's tractor driven by his hired man. Unsurprisingly, he offered us a ride on that tractor. You'll have to remember there were absolutely no laws against a vehicle like that carrying more than the driver back then and Bob's offer was simply kind and neighborly to two young lads.

So we piled on. Bob on the seat, me on his lap, and my brother Ken on the full fender that covered the wheel and prevented mud from flying up as it moved along in its "road gear," which could accomplish up to 12 miles per hour or so. But he wasn't "wide open" on the rutty, slippery road, and had me sitting between him and the steering wheel, which impacted, no doubt, his level of control of the machine on the slippery, rutted road. And that lack of control would have contributed to what was about to happen. We came to a fairly high grade through what at times was a slough holding up to a foot or two of water; we had seen it like that umpteen times. On this occasion, after a dry spell, and fortunately so, there was no water, just soft, mushy, grassy ground.

The Ancient Path

And there, as we crossed this high grade, for some reason, the right front wheel had crawled out of the shallow rut created by traffic during muddy days, and was going over the edge of the embankment. Bob cranked the wheel sharply left to try to bring the tractor back onto the road. It caught, and flipped us. I cannot remember any sensation of the turnover; all I can remember is being squished between the steering wheel and the seat and the fender of the upside-down tractor. How Bob and Ken had been thrown off, I cannot imagine. At any rate, they were free of the upset; I was the only one under the tractor, which was sitting in the soft ditch, all four tires in the air, and resting on fenders, steering wheel, engine hood, and a broken exhaust stack! But not with its full weight on me, or I'd have been history!

Some part of me was exposed; a very panicked Bob had me by the hand, I think, which he could reach, trying to pull me free, not knowing how badly I was injured. He was pulling hard, calling to me, "C'mon, Lolly! C'mon, Lolly!" Did I mention I hated being called Lolly? It's not close to Lawrence, or to Larry, which I could handle! I was entirely unaware that the position I was in was impossible! How could I have been sitting on Bob's lap, and yet HE HAD BEEN THROWN FREE, as had Ken, and both were uninjured! And I was the one jammed underneath. I didn't waste time pondering the fact that I should be dead, and I wriggled in response to Bob's pulling, and his trying to lift the 3400-pound tractor by its fender. His lifting accomplished little, but it seemed my wriggling did! Nor did I ponder how fortunate we were that there happened to be no water in the slough; the spring thaw had created a slough, but there was no longer any water. I realized that the soft earth was allowing me some wiggle room, and I kept wriggling. It occurs to me at this very moment that I record this, that Bob's frantic efforts to lift the tractor may not have been totally ineffective. Since the tractor was in fact on level ground now, and the main weight of the machine would have been on the fenders and the crushed STEERING WHEEL and engine hood, a central point, the machine could have rocked the tiniest bit as Bob desperately lifted. Ken may have been helping, too. He was totally unhurt, as Bob apparently was. All I knew was—I wanted OUT OF THERE! And I was making progress—the soft earth very forgiving. I have no idea how long it took, but eventually I was free, and I don't remember a single bruise or painful part on my body! So we just carried on walking to school. I have no idea how they righted the tractor. It would not have been damaged beyond repair.

No one knows better than I, how unlikely was my escape alive, much less uninjured! Had it happened when there was water in that ditch—my children would never have been born!

The story is not over. There is an epilog. About twelve years or so after that incident, I was reminded how miraculous my survival of the tractor accident was—how I was the beneficiary of a gift from my heavenly Father in that I had been granted survival in that incident. I shouldn't have survived it, but He had to have stepped in. Everything said I should have died, but I escaped totally uninjured!

The epilog: A friend and I had been putting in time before attending a local dance, listening to my car radio. Somehow, I don't recall how, we got information that there had just been an accident south of our home town. We knew only that there had been an accident, and that someone had called for a tow truck. We drove out in that direction, following the tow truck. Several miles along a gravel road, there was activity.

As we drew closer, I felt a wave of shivers go through my body —a tractor, very similar to the one in which I had escaped, was resting on hood and fenders, in a very shallow ditch. It was a Massey-Harris 30, very much a modern version of the 101! We could see little at first, it being evening. The tow truck had been followed by an ambulance, and my friend and I were available to help them pull out the tractor operator when the machine was raised slightly. It was immediately apparent that he was deceased; his head had been crushed in the upset. You can imagine what flashed through my mind! Why was I able to survive what could certainly have been my death? Only God knows.

None of us really know how many times we may have been in a situation where our lives could have ended, given a tiny differential in times of arrival somewhere, or choices we made to do this, or that, simple everyday decisions which can have an impact out of all proportion to the decision itself. And yet the moment passed with

The Ancient Path

NO IMPACT WHATEVER on our lives. Such was the case when, between the escape from the tractor upset and the occasion of recognizing how blessed I had been, and having for the most part completely forgotten the straw pile blunder, when another incident occurred.

My brother and I and a friend serving as a temporary farm hand were out on a completely unpleasant but very necessary task in that area of Saskatchewan, boring and tiring, but not in any way to be considered dangerous. It was the task of stone-picking. Our farm was quite typical for the area, in that our home quarter, once the original prairie had been broken for planting, seemed to literally **grow** stones. So stone-picking was a necessary part of preparing a field for planting, for the reason that they could cause damage to farm equipment, or, when a portion of a field was thickly littered with rocks even the size of apples, or even a football, the seed couldn't be planted evenly because of the machinery's inability to penetrate the soil. Our home quarter-section of land was particularly infested; they seemed to propagate like gophers; every year there were new stones revealed. My brother and I made no secret of the fact that we didn't really enjoy this task, and on one occasion I remember reminding my easy-going but conscientious father that we thought there were other ways to handle this task.

As a matter of fact, others had had the same revelation, and a machine called a "stone-picker" had just recently come on the market. It was drawn along by a farm tractor, with a small, heavy-duty reel equipped with heavy iron fingers, a bucket into which the reel would sweep the stones, and a hydraulic dumping cylinder (if indeed the tractor was equipped to use hydraulics). Unaware of our limitations, though, and unfazed by the complications, on one occasion of stone-picking with Dad and my brother using the same old horse-and-wagon technology, I presumed to bring up the matter with Dad: "Dad, how come you don't get a rock-picker, huh? We have more stones on this dumb farm than anybody else. We never really get 'em picked up. Seems like rocks grow on this land. Did you know, Dad, that Earl Croswell's just bought a rock-picker! Why don't you get one, huh? Why don't you get a rock-picker, Dad?" Dad's answer was brief: "I got TWO!"

So out rock-picking Ken and Ian and I had gone, a placid team of horses pulling a wooden-wheeled wagon with a low, sturdy box into which we typically loaded the stones one by one, the horses dozing at the stops, always ready to move ahead on command. We hadn't gone far this day, however, when we decided to hit a different area, a bit down the field and on the other side of a ravine down which water would run in the spring, or after a strong shower. Not that there was a shortage of rocks anywhere, but hey—"Put the pain off as long as you could!" may have been our rationale for the move. The horses moved briskly along, all three of us standing in macho postures, riding the rough wagon with skillful balance, though, in the low-walled box, there was nothing to hold on to. But real men learn to do that, so away we went down the field toward the still-stonier bit of land.

We came to the lip of the rather sharp dip, and the horses, pushed by the wagon, allowed themselves to be pushed to gallop speed as they hit the bottom of the ravine and, as horses do, to use the momentum to help them up the coming hill. For some reason, perhaps seeing something we didn't, part way up the other side of the ravine, they swerved suddenly, and I, unprepared for the direction change, went over the side of the box to land on my face behind the front wheel of the wagon, and in front of the rear wheel. How was there adequate time for me to hit the ground before the rear wheel hit me? That escapes me to this day. No matter how I reconstruct it, I couldn't see it possible to wind up where I did. But hit the ground face first, I did, and the rear wheel ran over my rear end, along my back, and bounced off my head, to land a foot or so beyond the imprint of my face in the fortunately soft dirt of the field! Fortunately there was not a load of stones in the box. Fortunately, too, not one of the spokes of the iron-tired, many-spoked wheels caught a part of my body to tear me to pieces at the speed this all happened. Proof of what happened was as plain as the nose on my face—actually, as plain as the imprint in the dirt that told the story.

Ian got the horses stopped at the top of the hill and they ran down to where I raised my face from the dust, my mouth full of dirt, and feeling a bit shaken up, expecting to find blood pouring—but—

there was nothing, just a small knot on the back of my head, beginning to grow a bit. The evidence, however, was there, but the escape almost unscathed still unbelievable. In the dirt lay drawn the story: the imprint of my prone body clearly drawn in the fortunately soft dirt, the track of the rear wheel, interrupted where it climbed my rump, squarely in the middle of my back, then no mark except that of my prone body, and then the return of the wheel to the ground about 12 inches beyond the imprint of my face in the blessedly soft and dusty earth, which spoke of the speed at which all this had happened.

Ken came running back to the cadaver he'd no doubt expected to find, just as I raised my dust-filled mouth to spit out the dirt, and he couldn't help laughing. I'd been wearing a cap; it had been shaken off, but other than that, I was able to rise from the dirt, brush myself off, and resume our stone-picking task. I wasn't even bleeding.

Why, I ask still, thinking about this event ... why did I not get tangled, arms and legs flying as they must have been, in the spokes of the wheel, to be torn from my body? How did I have time to fall into the space behind the front wheel and ahead of the rear wheel, and hit the ground before the rear wheel arrived? There would only have been a space of about five feet between the rear rim of the front wheel and the forward rim of the rear wheel, and yet I'd had time to hit the ground before the rear wheel had hit me. Physics says it would have been impossible—but there it was, in the picture in the dirt. How handy, how fortuitous, that in a field so littered with stones, not a one of them was there to re-design my face as the heavy, metal-rimmed wooden wheel carrying the weight of the wagon, box, and 300 lbs of passengers made its way across my prone body? How did I have time to FALL ABOUT FOUR FEET AND BE FLAT ON MY FACE before the rear wheel of a wagon weighing roughly 1000 pounds rolled over my body? How handy, how fortuitous? How "lucky?" How about: HOW MIRACULOUS? Add this: I'd been standing with my BACK to the side of the box over which I had fallen. How did I NOT land on my back, have the wheel hit my jaw, and run over my face? One might chuckle and say that would have had to be an improvement, but the fact remains: Someone had His mighty hand on me all the way to the ground! Someone **rescued** me from … who knows? So we rushed back to the house, got in the car and drove to town to have me checked out? NOT! We went on stone-picking. I had a bit of an egg on my head but was not severely hampered for the work.

This event resonates with me more than ever as I pile on the years. I can think of several more events where I escaped possible injury, but in some cases they were at least partially the result of errors in judgment I made—ill-advised decisions. But these episodes are the hardest to discount—SOMEONE had to have His hand on me. "Thank You, my Lord and Savior!"

As I read these accounts of my father, I can't help bawling, moved with both love for my dad, and gratefulness to my Lord. By all rights he should have been killed on multiple occasions, and I, my brothers and sisters, my nieces and nephews, and my own children should not have even existed. But that was not God's plan. I am a part of God's plan. My family is a part of God's plan. He will protect us, keep us, and bring to pass everything He has planned for our lives, until that day when He will call us home. He is the Almighty One, the All Powerful One, the Sovereign One over life and death.

Update:

It was interesting to note that the Lord healed my fear of winter—I still don't like it, but I am no longer afraid of it—directly before the Canadian prairies entered the coldest winter in eighty years, with many, many nights, and some days, registering more than forty degrees Celsius below zero. God is good!

O Lord,
You are the Alpha and Omega, the First and the Last, the Beginning and the End. In You, Lord, I will put my trust. Your goodness goes before those who fear You.

The Ancient Path

Lord, there have been times in my life when I have felt weak, helpless, and vulnerable. An uneasy, unrelenting wariness grips my soul with the threat of things out of my control, when I realize that I cannot, *will not*, ever have control over them. But Lord, You have ultimate control over them. You are sovereign, and You reign supreme. God, I repent for not trusting You with that sovereignty over my life. I repent for partnering with doubt, fear, and mistrust, not fully believing that You can keep me and my loved ones safe in all circumstances. I turn from operating under the controlling spirit in attempt to do the things only You can truly do.

I repent for partnering with death and destruction in any form. I come out of alignment with them. I choose to partner with life and the creativity of God in every aspect of my being. I bind up all spirits of fear and doubt and step into alignment with the knowledge that You have dominion over the heavens and the earth, and over my life. Expose any lies that have been planted in my mind that have allowed fear to grow, and pull out any roots that have been established. Reveal any events or circumstances that have opened this spiritual door. Heal any trauma that has resulted because of it.

Forgive me for my lack of faith. Release that depth of peace into my life only You can give. Let me walk always full of Your grace and confidence, that Your light may shine through me to all man. I humbly pray this in the mighty name of our Lord and Savior, Jesus Christ.

The Ancient Path

Connect the Dots:

_____

_____

_____

_____

_____

_____

_____

_____

_____

_____

_____

_____

_____

_____

_____

_____

_____

17. WEAR WHITE

If you love Me, keep My
commandments.

John 14:15

'If you will walk in My ways,
And if you will keep My command,
Then you shall also judge My house,
And likewise have charge of My courts;
I will give you places to walk
Among these who stand here.

Zechariah 3:7

Strategy to Implement

Pass your tests. Be obedient—even if you don't know or understand the purposes behind what God is asking of you.

Wear no makeup.

It wasn't a thought or a voice—more of an awareness building within me as I sat at the table during the conference's complimentary breakfast; like something I suspected may end up happening. By the time I left later that morning, I *knew* I would not be wearing any makeup when I returned that evening, much to my chagrin. And I had no idea as to why that was required of me. It wasn't that I wore a lot; I often skipped it all together in the summer. However, for evening events in public, I feel more comfortable with it on.

Over the course of the afternoon, the expanse of this notion grew. My ring and earrings were next. I was to take them off. Then came the stripping off of all nail polish. And again, I didn't know why, I just had a sense that that was what I was to do. It was not rational, or logical, nor really needed in my opinion, but I felt the

Lord was asking it of me for some unknown reason—and that was enough for me. Even if it wasn't Him, I didn't want to take the chance of being disobedient. I knew this was a season where God wanted us to pass our tests—not for His benefit, but for ours.

A spontaneous shopping trip was required to meet the next directive I felt bubbling up, as I did not have anything appropriate:

Wear White

This was followed by an unplanned stop at the carwash to make the vehicle I had been borrowing for the last few months (would you believe it was white?) shiny and clean. Not sure what was transpiring, I asked the Lord why I had to strip off all my makeup, nail-polish and jewelry, wear white, and ensure my white vehicle had no dirt on it as I drove back to the conference—and did I really need to do this? It was sort of embarrassing to appear in public *stripped down*—much like running into that person you haven't seen in a long time when you have just popped out to the store quickly before getting ready for the day, hoping you won't see anyone you know.

Was the Lord wanting me to make public repentance on behalf of myself, someone else, or even a people group? Was I a symbolic sacrifice? Was I representing the Bride of Christ? I had no idea, and received no response, other than this *knowing* that I was not to worry about what others would think (fear of man), and honor God by being obedient in what I knew by then had come from Him (fear of God).

During one of the worship songs I had dropped to my knees, and soon words about *wearing white* rang out, and I felt an intense connection to the Lord. Other than that, there was no "big moment" where I felt anything had happened. There was a time for testimonies, and though I had a lot of stories of what the Lord was doing in my life I could have shared, I did not feel led to take the microphone.

Walking out to the parking lot that night, I questioned God, not with doubt but with curiosity, as to the purpose behind the whole production tied to that evening. Though I did not receive any direct response, I still trusted God knew what He was doing even if I did not, and that though nothing apparently had happened in the natural realm, perhaps something had transpired in the spiritual realm of which I was yet unaware. And more importantly, I was obedient. I had passed my test, even though I hadn't really known what the test was about.

One week later, the Lord showed me this Scripture:

> For the LORD had said to Moses, "Say to the children of
> Israel, 'You *are* a stiff-necked people. I could come up
> into your midst in one moment and consume you. Now
> therefore, take off your ornaments, that I may know what
> to do to you.' " So the children of Israel stripped
> themselves of their ornaments by Mount Horeb.
>
> ***Exodus 33:5-6***

Or, as the New Living Translation expresses it, "Remove your jewelry and fine clothes while I decide what to do with you." Still not knowing what it meant in my specific context, it was reassuring that it was indeed the sort of thing the Lord had people do.

Several weeks later, at *Trading Floors: Unlocking the Wealth From the Courts of Heaven* with Robert Henderson, he referred to a "point of obedience." This reference referred to rather "interesting" things the Lord had people do simply in obedience to Him. Whether or not my *stripping down* had any spiritual significance or was a point of obedience, I'll perhaps never know. But I don't have to know or understand. I had passed my test. In that, I am certain.

Let's pray, and ask for strength to pass all of our tests.

The Ancient Path

Dear Lord,

You have purchased me with Your blood. That is everything—it is the only thing. Though I can never repay You with anything I have, I can offer everything I have, everything I am. I long to be one of Your remnant people. I want to be a son of God, the ones led by Your spirit. I wish to walk in the fullness of Christ living in me. But above all, my desire is to please You. I want to obey Your commands and follow Your ways. And that means I need to be obedient. I need to take the steps You place in front of me. I need to go wherever You lead me, and do all You ask, without question, without fear, without fail. Teach me how to hear Your voice so clearly that I will know all You ask of me. Please grant me the courage and fortitude I need to walk it out, no matter how steep the path or how long the road.

Please deliver me from fear of man. Bind up any rebellion lingering in my soul. Expose any roots of bitterness that hinder an unwavering walk with You. I ask You to instill in me a reverent fear that will keep me choosing You over pleasing man, or attempting to fulfill my own selfish desires. I want to be entrenched so firmly on the path You have for me that nothing will cause me to stray. I long to be faithful with every part of my life. I know You only need my willingness in order to work through me, bringing Heaven to Earth. I put my will on the altar, Lord, and offer it unto You. Thank you for Jesus, in whose precious name I can pray.

The Ancient Path

Connect the Dots:

_____

_____

_____

_____

_____

_____

_____

_____

_____

_____

_____

_____

_____

_____

_____

_____

18. JUMPING BACKWARD

Trust in the LORD with all your heart,

And lean not on your own understanding;

In all your ways acknowledge Him,

And He shall direct your paths.

Proverbs 3:5-6

"Blessed *is* she who believed,

for there will be a fulfillment of those things

which were told her from the Lord."

Luke 1:45

Strategy to Implement

Do what it takes to deepen your trust in Him. It is then He can take you to unimaginable heights. The sky is the limit.

Jumping ... backward ... off a cliff should be no different than stepping off a sidewalk curb. We should trust the Lord that much—even when we can't see where we are going, or if He is there to catch us. It's getting to that place of trust that is so very difficult. My prod from the Lord to begin that journey started with a sense the Lord was going to release time for me to write. Being the sole bread-winner for myself and two kids made the prospect of cutting back from full-time work a little unnerving. But as I calculated the feasibility of this possibility, including all the financial resources I would have access to, I determined that eighty percent of my current hours would give me both time to write and still meet my financial obligations.

And that is when I started feeling a strong tugging in my spirit that it was *more* He wanted—or perhaps *less* is the better term: "*Am I to go as low as half-time?*" was the question I fervently penned in my journal early one morning at a conference. To deepen my trust in Him, to know I could count on Him for everything I needed, it would take more than doing something I could do on my own; I would have to be placed in a position of utter dependency on Him for every aspect of my journey. Only I didn't know at the time that this was what this road was to be about. Yes, writing, but oh, so much more!

My undeniable answer came later that day through the words of a prophetically gifted man, at a ministry time I had had no intention of attending. I had ducked out of the conference to support a friend at her book launch, when another friend called, asking if I was able to "give her backup" at the prophetic ministry session for the very conference I had just left, as it was her first time. Unable to be in two places at once, I let her know I'd see if it worked out, not truly thinking it would. However, within a short period of time, I inexplicably became so fatigued I could not keep my eyes open. Disappointed I could no longer be a support to either of my friends, and profusely apologizing to the one, I left. Physically holding my eyelids open on the Ring Road, I drove home.

As I reached the turnoff from the highway, the overwhelming tiredness left as quickly as it had come—and left me with a choice to make. Did I go straight home anyway, or was God telling me something? The strange happenings seemed suspiciously like the workings of the Lord! If I chose to, I could easily make it back to the conference in plenty of time to meet my friend and provide her with the prayer support she had requested. Not wanting to ignore what I now figured was divine guidance, I joined their prophetic team and ministered to all who were seated in our chair. I just didn't know that I too, would be one in that chair. As I gathered my belongings to make my exit, one of my prayer partners declared something to the effect that I could not leave until he gave me the word God had for me.

Prophetic Word - March 2016 (abridged)

I am just going to give it right to you. <u>The word God gave me for you was, "Yes!" And it was a bright, bold, shining "Yes!"</u> I see you standing in front of a door and you are like, "Do I do this? Do I walk through this door? What do I do? Ahhhh! Is this You, God? What is this?" You are scared, but on the other side of the door, I see Jesus open the door. He said, "Come on in. It's Okay. Yes. It's okay."

And on the other side of the door there was a table set for two. It was as you walked into the will and purpose that God has called you to, He wants to take you to a deeper—a love relationship with Him.

And this door you are going through is like a changing of season. You are going from one thing to the next. And it is very clear that this is a new thing. It's a deeper relationship. It's a trust relationship. There has been trust broken in your life, and God is saying, *"I am healing that for you. I am going to be the One in your life that you can trust and that you know that I've got you. I won't harm you. My plans are to prosper you, to see good things in your life."*

The Ancient Path

You are going into a season where you are walking closer with Him. You are going into a deeper relationship with Him, but there is more for you. There is just more for you in the area of relationship and just time.

—Jeff Barnhardt

The only *Yes/No* question I had recently asked of the Lord, and had, in fact, written down, as I had said, *that very morning*, was if I was to work half-time. "Yes." There was no other possible context for this word. It was plain and simple. Only not so simple. I had to either believe God and **all** He was telling me, **all** He wanted me to do, **all** He had for me, or walk away from it all. And so scared and tentatively, as tentative as one can be when jumping off a cliff—backwards—I jumped. I could not forsake Him, nor what He was asking of me. I had to trust that He would be there to catch me. I had to know that He would be the One to keep the roof over our heads, and the food on our plates.

Sometime in March, I let my administration know I would be forfeiting my full-time contract, electing to work fifty percent. Though I wasn't quite sure how my expenses would be paid, I trusted it was the Lord's leading, and His plans for me were good. Two months later I would receive an out-of-the-blue phone call, offering me my first writing contract. I was yet unknown, but the Lord, he had said, had led him to offer it to me, sight unseen. (He really had to trust the Lord—he didn't even know I was a writer!) And month by month, my needs were miraculously met. Some months were "more interesting" than others, but nonetheless, somehow, someway, He came through for me every time.

The adventure continued the following year. Only this time, all external resources depleted, I needed an even stronger confirmation. I did not want to go outside of the Lord's will, but I also had responsibilities to my family. I had to know it was Him leading me. While praying over this decision, the Lord showed me a picture of a bridge. It started on one side and ended on the other like a normal bridge, but where the middle of the bridge should have been was only an open expanse of water. I knew the promises of God lay on the other side of the bridge, and getting there was to be a walk of faith.

To me, the picture meant teaching only half-time again, and continuing on my road of writing, editing, and spending much time in communion with the Lord—all of which also meant being in a situation of dependency on Him, especially now, after already coming through a year on a greatly reduced income. But the decision was still too big. I could not put everything on the line again without knowing beyond all doubt that this was His plan for me. Thankfully, He was not yet done speaking to my heart. Not twenty minutes later, I received a text from a friend. I am not sure where it was from, but it spoke the needed message, loud and clear!

The Ancient Path

"God is already ahead of you putting bridges and steps for your safety and direction along your way. Where there is no bridge, the water will divide. Have faith, step toward the promise and keep moving forward. God's glory goes before you and His glory guards you from behind." (Source unknown)

… And so I jumped once again. And once again, He was faithful. And that was round two. (There are many stories to tell of this two-and-a-half-year adventure, but that is for another book!)

The jump for round three was a little more severe, a little more complete. I could still have reclaimed my full-time contract after the two-year absence, including all the benefits of the health plan—a deal not always easy to come by, especially when you love the position. However, it was not to be. The Lord asked me, instead, to lay down my career of twenty-two years and walk into the unknown. It should have been harder than the first two jumps, but since my level of trust in the Lord had grown exponentially, all that was required this time was His slight nudge, and over I went. The nudge looked like this:

Previously, while praying over the direction of our lives with a friend, though not about this specific situation, I felt we were to cut our parachute strings and free-fall off a cliff backwards. Not fully understanding at the time what this meant, nor the ramifications of this decision, we were obedient, and prophetically snipped the strings, leaving our lives in the hands of the Lord. I had learned, through the adventures of the past two years, how to be dependent on Him for everything. I had become very grateful for everything He has given me, and everywhere He has taken me on my journey. And I knew, beyond a shadow of a doubt, that I could trust Him. He's got me. I would follow where He leads. Even if it meant jumping off a metaphoric cliff. As in the words of Mary:

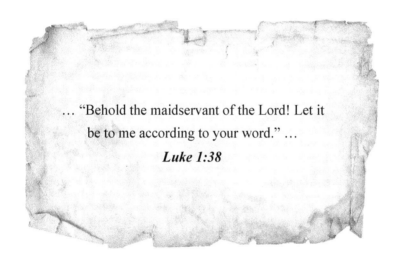

… "Behold the maidservant of the Lord! Let it
be to me according to your word." …
Luke 1:38

Not too many days later, while praying with another friend about "a monumental decision" I had to make (I did not inform her of any details), after our prayer she said something to the effect that the

Lord's hands are there to catch me, but for some reason I can't see them …

"Yes, that's because I am jumping *backwards*!" I laughed. What other response was there?

"Oh … and for some reason," she continued, "I see … a parachute!"

Would you allow me the honor of praying with you? (Maybe nudge you off a cliff?) Let's come before the Lord and request of Him what He has for you.

Dear Lord,

You know the story of my book, start to finish. You know every path I need to walk to raise me up to the heights to which You want to take me. I seem to forget that sometimes. And You love me beyond measure. When You ask the difficult things of me, it is not to punish me—no, it is the contrary—it is to strengthen me, perfect me, make me into Your likeness. It is to draw me in closer and closer to You. It is to form a trust bond so deep I know to my core that You will not leave me, forsake me, or fail me. With You, I can do all things.

I repent for not trusting You. I repent for allowing fear to make me doubt Your motives, Your ways, Your wisdom, Your guidance. Please forgive me. I want to be able to jump off tall towers, knowing You will catch me. I want to walk into the water, over my head, knowing there is nothing to fear as You are by my side.

The Ancient Path

Lord, stir up any areas in which I have not trusted You; perhaps have even locked those areas away deep in my heart, in hopes of burying them forever, never to be touched. Lord, I give You access to those areas. I invite You into every area of my life to sift, and to hold me accountable. Go deep, Lord, deeper than I have ever allowed You to go. The time is now. I want to move forward into all You have for me. I know the road You choose for me would not be the one I would choose for myself—it is the harder, narrower road. But Lord, I choose it—I choose You and following You, above all else. Take me to that road, the narrow one, the high one, the one You want me on, and with my hand in Yours, I'll jump …

Obedience is the key that unlocks doors.
—Kimm Reid

Yet indeed I also count all things loss for the excellence of the knowledge of Christ Jesus my Lord, for whom I have suffered the loss of all things, and count them as rubbish, that I may gain Christ.
Philippians 3:8

If you are not firm in the faith, you will not be firm at all.
Isaiah 7:9b (ESV)

The Ancient Path

Connect the Dots:

_____

_____

_____

_____

_____

_____

_____

_____

_____

_____

_____

_____

_____

_____

_____

_____

_____

19. POISON

And he said, "Bring me a new bowl, and put salt in it." So they brought *it* to him. Then he went out to the source of the water, and cast in the salt there, and said, "Thus says the LORD: 'I have healed this water; from it there shall be no more death or barrenness.' "

2 Kings 2:20-21

> # Strategy to Implement
>
> **Trust the Lord to show you what to pray, how to pray, even if it seems contradictory, out of the ordinary (or perhaps even a little strange).**

I'm grateful I had read the life or death text from my friend before I had hopped into my vehicle. Her friend's little girl had been transported to the hospital in another city, and was fighting for her life. They did not know what was wrong with her. Stunned and at a loss as to what to pray, I cried out to God.

Suddenly, I had a strong sense *she had gotten into something that was poison to her body*. Those were the exact words that worked their way into my mind. I started praying in that direction, but then received another text. The doctors were thinking it was perhaps some sort of bacterial infection. I acknowledged this new information in my head, but in my spirit I still felt like she needed to have poison removed from her body. It was killing her. At one point her lips were blue. She had stopped breathing.

Following that spur in my spirit, I asked the Lord what to do. She had to have the poison removed from her body. That was all I knew. I started repeatedly sucking in every ounce of air my lungs would take, picturing the poison being sucked out, then exhaling as hard as I could, making sure every bit of that poison was out of me as well. By this time, having had to be on my way, I was driving down the street and rather glad to have been alone. It would have been hard to explain this one! Over and over again, I would inhale and exhale as powerfully as possible, praying for God to remove the toxic substance trying to steal her little life. (And praying I would not pass out …)

Several hours later I found out the doctors had been wrong. The two-year-old had accidentally ingested medication—*poison to her body*. Knowing now what it was, the doctors were able to save her. But I know it was God's grace, mercy, and wisdom that had saved her. He had taken the poison from her body and gave her life.

Four days later, I saw this little girl running around the room, like nothing had happened—like she had not been on her death bed, lips blue, fighting for her life.

Update:

Thankfully, this particular story of the little girl ends on a happy note. I thought the chapter would end there too, and for many months, it did. But it was not to be so in the final draft. Recently, I had run into a friend who had had an encounter with another who most likely did not speak the nicest, uplifting things over her and her life. I felt something was spiritually put in her or spilled over her. On the way to my vehicle, I casually mentioned we had to be sure to get together to pray to take it off—whatever *it* was. I had been busy—in a hurry to meet up with some others, and I had WALKED AWAY. I found out later she had been hospitalized within two days with a *kidney infection* of some sort, with an unknown cause. Our *kidney* filters out *poison* in our bodies. Lesson learned. Those were not the best dots to have had to connect. Sorry, Friend. Sorry, Lord.

It is so important to pray, always and in all ways. Come, join with me in prayer to the Almighty.

Wow, Lord!
Your hand moving among us amazes me! Your wonders never cease! You put Your very hand upon ours to guide us into Your works. Let me trust Your guidance. Open my spirit to hear Yours. Thank you that as I listen to Your heart, I hear it beat for others. Teach me, show me, train me. I am open to all You have for me and others through me. There is no higher stake than the lives of those You put in my path.

I am sorry for the times I have missed Your word to me, Your directive to me, out of my own lack of understanding, busyness, or even selfishness. Let me always take the time and make the effort to respond to what You show me. Choose me, Lord! Send me!

I ask for the strength and courage to always step out into what You are calling me to do. Keep me close enough to Your breath that

I know it is from You. I ask for more and more discernment, increasing in depth as I show myself faithful. Keep me ever aware of Your voice speaking, guiding, training, loving, keeping. Thank you that even one such as I, can partner with You to bring Heaven to Earth. Thank you for choosing to do miracles through my hands. Thank you for honoring me as I honor You. I pray these things in the life-giving name of Jesus Christ.

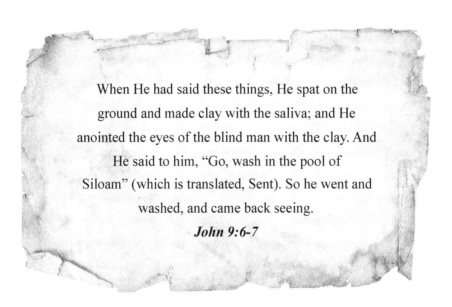

When He had said these things, He spat on the ground and made clay with the saliva; and He anointed the eyes of the blind man with the clay. And He said to him, "Go, wash in the pool of Siloam" (which is translated, Sent). So he went and washed, and came back seeing.

John 9:6-7

The Ancient Path

Connect the Dots:

_____

_____

_____

_____

_____

_____

_____

_____

_____

_____

_____

_____

_____

_____

_____

_____

_____

20. TIMELESS

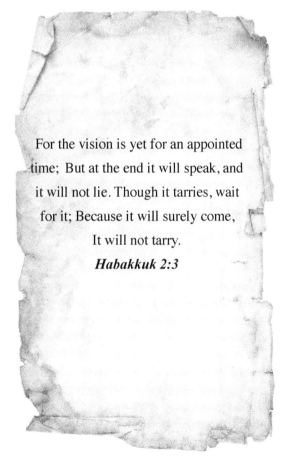

For the vision is yet for an appointed
time; But at the end it will speak, and
it will not lie. Though it tarries, wait
for it; Because it will surely come,
It will not tarry.

Habakkuk 2:3

Strategy to Implement

Don't limit God's plans for you by hanging on to timelines as you understand them to function.

God transcends time. He is not limited nor defined by time; He has no beginning and no end. He had set our destiny before time even began (2 Timothy 1:9). This deems timelines as we think we understand them to be, irrelevant.

Recently, the Lord asked me to read back through my journals from the last three years, focusing on His words to me. (That's a lot of journals, Lord!) But as I started to read through them, revelation dawned. Though some of them were *now* assignments at the time, many of the words He spoke to me back then had not been in reference to the present, but for a time more than three years later— or more, for the ones that spoke of things still to come. (The Bible itself is like that. Words written were relevant for the people at the time, but are still playing out in the world today—just the names are different.)

With everything that had transpired in my life in the meantime, and in conjunction with the knowledge I had gained since I had first heard and recorded those words from Him, I now saw them from a different perspective. I had new understandings of them. Their meanings shifted, changed, and grew in depth, as I now could see how some of the things had come to fulfillment, and how others had a new foundation on which to be built—a foundation that had not existed at the time I had previously heard Him whisper them to my heart.

Some of the things I had thought were to occur *soon* in my limited definition of the term, I now understand were words of preparation. Just as God had shared part of His plans with Abraham, Noah, and Joseph in preparation for what was to come—sometimes many, many years in advance—He still gives us those same kinds of words to ready our hearts, prepare our minds, and develop our character so we can walk in His calling for us. He does *not*, however, tend to share *all* of His plans ahead of time, because they may seem too big or too hard for us, or the training too treacherous, and we'd run the other way! We must remember, though, we will be the person we need to be to carry all He asks of us if we submit ourselves to His ways, and walk the ancient path He has laid out for us.

Expecting God's word and promises to be delivered according to our timelines only serves to breed confusion, discouragement, and disappointment. We must adhere to His and be patient as He places all the elements necessary to put His plan into motion.

Two of my friends found this concept to be true in their experiences. Both had received a word of prophecy and tucked the corresponding notes into their journals at the time. And both had the notes "fall out" of their journals, which had long since been filled and shelved, at the *exact moment* in time when the words had become *now* words. Another friend had also received a prophetic word which made no sense to her at the time, as events that had not yet happened were in past tense. Twenty years later, as she cleaned her basement before entering into a new phase of her life, she rediscovered the transcribed pages of the word from so long ago. Amazingly, but not surprisingly, as she reread the word at this point in her life, *everything* that had been written in the past had already come to pass, and she was now stepping into the things that had spoken into her future. The original word had essentially not been given to her as her present-self, but for her future-self. God operates with inexplicable precision timing, even when we don't understand it or fathom how it could come to pass.

When we, as humans with a limited perspective, look back at an event that has already occurred, it is easy to see how everything fit together, or didn't fit, in its timing. In its simplest form, that is a reflection of how God operates. He is already in tomorrow and knows *what* is going to happen, *exactly when* it is going to happen. He knows what has to be aligned for things to come to pass as He has orchestrated. He knows the depth of character we need to possess to fulfill that which He has set out for us. We, on the other hand, don't know any of these things! Trusting Him in His timing, rather than trying to constrain Him within our ignorant timelines, is the choice of the wise.

Prophetic Word – July 2017 (abridged)

I felt like the Lord showed me where He is and there is no time there. I feel like He would say, "Get your eyes off of time. I don't deal in time. I don't work in time. I don't operate in time. I am concerned about you. My heart and My passion is for you as my daughter."

I see that He is trying to pull out from you a shard of this thing called *time* and the question you keep asking, "When, Lord, when?" But you are holding the shard. So He is asking you to let go of it so He can pull it out. There is nothing you need to do except let go of it. He is asking, "Do you trust Me in the timing of everything that you know is coming?" But nothing is going to move forward until He can remove that *time* element from you.

I see a shard of glass, but He is not going to yank it out. You think if you hold it tightly enough, it is not going to cut you because it won't move; but if you loosen your grip and He pulls, then it is going to cut you. But He is not asking you to loosen your grip, He is asking you to completely remove your hands from it so that He can have it and it won't cut you and it won't hurt. He is asking, "Do you trust Me enough to let go of time?"

The Lord says, "You need to know that I am in control of this. You are not in charge of it. You are not in control of it. All I want from you is your willingness and your trust of Me. So if I have those two things there is no limit to what I can do through you. There is nothing I cannot do through a person who is willing and who trusts Me to do things in M*y timing* when I want them done as I want them done.

"Everything is for your benefit. Everything is for your best. Even these things that seem a waste of time. They are not a waste of time. They are training for you. I am teaching you. I am training you. It is not for My benefit. I don't need to know all of this stuff. I already know this stuff. I live in it; it is all around me. I am in your yesterday and I am in your today and I am in your tomorrow. So just rest in Me. I have you in My hand. I am already in your future. Keep your eyes on Me and believe and trust that in every single situation and circumstance, whether it is amazing or whether it is really hard, always thank Me for it because I am training you in it to do what I see you doing right now in that moment, which is what I am in, which you are not there yet, but believe Me, I am already there. Let go of time. Don't worry about time because it is a prison. Just be in the moment; be in today. Anticipate tomorrow but don't go there; don't be there. Just be here today; and everyday is today, so don't ever worry about tomorrow and don't try to put yourself in tomorrow, just do today. Then tomorrow, do today. Then the next day, do today. Everyday is today."

—Kimm Reid

Can we let go of the glass shard of time together? Let's pray.

Dear Lord,

You are the great I Am, the Everlasting Father, the Creator of every living thing. In You I live, I breathe, I have my being. Without You I would be nothing—there would be nothing. Lord, take my hand as I walk with You, in Your steps, in Your timing; for Your timing transcends everything. There is nothing You do not know, cannot conceive, cannot bring about. Thank you for being in my today and in my tomorrow. Thank you for giving me the strength to live in the *now* moment, the moment You give me today, without being anxious about what is to come. I give You my willingness and I give You my trust, Lord. I will keep my eyes on You.

I repent for daring to think I know better than You in any situation or circumstance, about anyone or anything. I turn from trying to constrain, to limit You within my selfish, ignorant timelines. Who am I to question, to doubt, to be impatient, when Your wisdom is infinitely above mine—above all—and Your actions and plans are all done through the eyes of love? Lord, I let go, I let go! Take this glass shard called *time* out of my hand! I freely give it to You! I willfully place it at Your feet. Help me not to pick it up again, but release it time and time again!

Thank you for building a solid foundation in me through Your gift of time. Thank you for so conscientiously preparing me, readying my heart and developing my character so I am a fit vessel to carry the full calling You have planned for my life. Thank you that in Your timing, as I submit to Your will and Your ways, I will be the person I need to be, ready to carry the destiny You have placed upon my life. I pray this in the sovereign name of Jesus. Amen.

Connect the Dots:

_____

_____

_____

_____

_____

_____

_____

_____

_____

_____

_____

The Ancient Path

21. "CHOOSE ME!"

Then Jesus was led up by the Spirit into the wilderness to be tempted by the devil. And when He had fasted forty days and forty nights, afterward He was hungry.

Matthew 4:1-2

Then the disciples came to Jesus privately and said, "Why could we not cast it out?" So Jesus said to them, "Because of your unbelief; for assuredly, I say to you, if you have faith as a mustard seed, you will say to this mountain, 'Move from here to there,' and it will move; and nothing will be impossible for you. However, this kind does not go out except by prayer and fasting."

Matthew 17: 19-21

Strategy to Implement

Changing your language opens the door to God's partnership. Answer the call to fast. It changes you —takes you into the depths.

Staying in the shadows until the Lord calls you forth. ~~Fame~~. Giving every dime He asks you to give. ~~Fortune~~. Consecrating and sanctifying yourself unto the Lord. ~~Lust~~. Through trials and turmoil and tough times, learning to trust Him with every ounce of your being. ~~Fear~~. Laying down at His feet every crown He has given you. ~~Pride~~. As we align with God's ways on the ancient path, the enemy loses his grip of control over us; one by one these tools slip from his grasp, no longer effective. When we crucify the flesh, the enemy can no longer control or hinder us through the desires of the flesh. Yet for many of us, because we cannot completely abstain from it, food seems to linger as one of the remaining enticements. If Jesus is enough, should we be controlled by food?

When I first began fasting as a part of our ministry team protocol, I was adamant that a thick shake indeed counted as a liquid fast. It was my way of avoiding the discomfort of being hungry, and at the time, I didn't understand the tremendous value of biblical fasting. There seems to have been a trend of fasting items such as electronics, television, or social media. Those fasts are definitely needed, but I have found nothing else to have the same impact on my relationship with God, nor kill the flesh so effectively, than fasting from food. If you cannot be under enemy control over reputation, money, sex, fear, pride, or food, there are not too many weapons left in his arsenal.

The first fast I felt directly called to by the Lord was to stand with a friend during the final ten days of her forty-day fast. If she had been asked by the Lord to not eat for forty days and was obedient, who was I that I could not stand with her for the last ten? It was new territory, fasting more than three days on actual liquids, but the desire to be obedient to the Lord and the unwavering determination in my friend had been my inspiration to be faithful in this task. I felt I needed to put the fear of the Lord in action—obedience to Him trumping what I want or *did not want* to do.

I had found the first three days to have been uncomfortable, even painful—that gnawing in my belly so many times a day. But the Lord had reminded me of the hard roads of Ezekiel, Paul, Daniel, and Joseph. In light of their journeys, my temporary discomfort was not much for the Lord to ask of me. After three days, the physical battle had passed, my belly no longer crying out for sustenance, leaving only the mental battle to fight for the next week. Since I already followed a healthy eating plan, I did not have to undergo the caffeine/sugar detox that many new fasters experience. The headache produced at this time regretfully dissuades some from continuing their fast, not realizing that if they could endure the pain now, they could prevent disease later. (I challenge you to research the incredible health benefits of fasting. God not only wants us spiritually healthy, but physically as well!)

Several months later, I had woken up knowing I was to begin another fast. There is no other words to tell of it. I just knew if I ate, I would have been disobedient. Glancing at my calendar brought forth an immediate sensation that it was to be a two-week fast. When I went to mark the dates, I had noted that they had corresponded with the mission trip to Africa being sent from my church. Comprehension had dawned … I was to do my part in covering the team with prayer and fasting. Tremendous miracles and breakthrough had come forth during the trip—I was elated I had been faithful in playing my role, along with all those others He had called to be a part of that mission in some manner.

It had been interesting to note that after eleven days the Lord had released me from covering the African team, but had had me continue the fast, tightening it up to allow only water, (I even had to be careful not to swallow any toothpaste!) to accomplish a work within me. A Facebook post later that day had confirmed what I had sensed: the missionary itinerary in Africa had terminated, and the team was on to sightseeing!

It was somewhere in these times of fasting that I understood I had to stop saying, "I hate fasting!" but rather, metaphorically put my hand up and say, "Choose me, Lord! It is an honor that You would have me do this." In doing so, though it did not make the actual fast "easy," I believe it opened the door of opportunity to partner with the Lord on many occasions to bring Heaven to Earth, and this truly is a joy and an honor.

As the new year approached, I began to sense that I would be starting it with a fast; longer this time. In those last few days of December, the Lord had given me Daniel chapter 9 verse 3: "So I turned to the Lord God and pleaded with him in prayer and fasting" (NLT). I was drawn to circle the word "fasting," unaware that it was to be the first link in the soon-to-be-formed chain that would guide me along the path. As I sat at His feet listening, His words to me were: "Break down the strongholds as I show them to you. Follow My voice. It will grow stronger as your fast."

At some point that same morning, my sister sent me another Scripture on fasting. The evidence for beginning the new year with a thirty day fast was mounting. My journal reminds me that as I pulled out a book I had on fasting, those two very Scriptures were listed in Chapter One. I was persuaded … not overly excited … but fully persuaded. Let my journal tell the story:

Journal entry excerpts - December 2016

"Move forward, keep moving forward. Always move forward. Do not look back. See what I have in front of you, laid out before you, not behind you. Step into it, Jocelyn.

The Ancient Path

Do not look beside you. Look in front of you. This is where your focus needs to be. I am birthing something in you. It will be painful, but so worth it. Breathe through the pain.

Hang on to Me with both hands. Walk with Me through this. Do not try to figure it out. The ride is about to begin. It will be glorious. Trust Me, My child, trust Me. Always put your hand in Mine. I will lead the way. Stay in My presence. That is where the world makes its mistakes. It lets go of Me, gets distracted, tries to figure it out with human wisdom, thus limiting Me, robbing from Me, and assuming the glory for themselves. Always seek My direction. Always seek My instruction. Always seek My wisdom. Then you will be safe."

Lord, let me not waste or wish away even one minute of my life.

Lord, I seek Your wisdom, guidance, and instruction. Help me through this time. I wait on You for direction. I trust You.

Lord, my friend confirmed it will be a battle, but said You said I have all I need in Scripture. Please, Holy Spirit, remind me of what I need when I need it. Another said it is an important fast as I am being attacked before I even start. The enemy must not want this to happen.

Lord, teach me to abide in You in any areas in which I am not doing so ...

Help me to keep looking to You and breathing through the pain. Have Your way in this, Lord ...

Journal entry excerpts during the fast - January 2017

I feel my story will change this year—You are leading me to prepare for change.

I feel like I am to be resting up ... but I'm not sleeping ... it takes hours and hours to fall asleep ...

Lord, thank you that You have called me to this fast. Rough night. Praying for my flesh to bow down to my spirit and the Spirit of the Lord.

Perhaps saw a hand and a little girl with a basket in the shadows. They scare me when I see them, and I'm not really sure if I see them ... Makes my heart pound ... Yet ... I am curious about it. Not scared when awake ... just the "startle" of them. Texting with a friend:

The Ancient Path

And last night He told me this … it's for you as well as me. Keep your eyes on the end result. When an artist paints a picture, they keep their eyes on the picture in their mind, not on the canvas. If they thought after every brush stroke, "This isn't what I thought, this is ugly," they'd stop. How many masterpieces have never been created because the artist took his eye off the finished picture?

Hmmm …. so true … I keep thinking, What is the point … Then I get discouraged. It is so hard to keep going when you haven't seen any results.

Right. But you wouldn't tell people to walk on an unfinished bridge! It wouldn't be safe. So the Lord says this:
"While you are finishing the bridge, I am perfecting you. The way forward is through you trusting Me. I've not asked you to be responsible for the timing, only to be willing to come and build the bridge."

So pick up your torch and carry on. The Lord has given me a word for my situation and I give it to you and speak it over you … STEADFAST. You are STEADFAST.
(Look it up. It's great!)

207

Yup … unwavering. That was the word I had for you Monday. It all makes sense. Just so hard sometimes. I will pick up my torch/sword/cross aka pen and go on …

["Building the bridge" refers to the writing assignments the Lord had given me.]

DAY 6

Still hungry. Prayed with a friend. She said again, it's ok. I was <u>steadfast</u>. [Different friend, same word.] It is hard, but just have to keep going. Not nearly as bad as when I had my shoulder injury or when I was sick. That was worse … so I can do this.

[It was true. I had recognized that at other times in my life, I had been in more physical distress and mental battle than during the fast; the difference was, however, with the fast, I could end my "misery" by simply putting food in my mouth and swallowing—I had power and control over it, whereas the other times I had no choice but to walk through the pain. This aspect made it harder in a way—choosing between physical discomfort and obedience. This in itself brings a new dynamic into your spiritual growth. It takes you to new heights.]

The Ancient Path

Received a prophetic word last night:

Arise! Arise! Arise!

Your voice will rise up!

Do not let anyone muffle it from sounding off what needs to be expressed.

Grace & obedience seasoned with humility.

My love is enough; more than enough.

Expect unprecedented events in your life.

There is an opened door …

No one will be able to close it …

Lord, reading Leviticus and all the instruction they had to follow … Lord, we have it so easy next to them. I don't think we have a clue of hard life! I repent of being spoiled! I need to be a lot tougher! Lord, I need to have a revelation of Your majesty and Your greatness and Your love for me.

Thank you for the "assignment" to pray a blessing on my friend's church. After, she said how transformed I am. When she met me she thought how hollow I was; if someone flicked me with their finger, I'd shatter. Now, she is happy anytime I come. She is comforted with me just being there.

I was really struggling with my fast. My words kept being, "How am I going to get through this?" to the text message my friend sent me, about how I was "much stronger than I knew." It was from God for me. My thinking had to change to, "I am stronger than I know. With God I can do it."

I prayed in the spirit ... [a lot].

I also have to shift from looking ahead at how many more days I have to fast, and just focus on today, knowing God's mercies are new every morning for the day at hand.

DAY 9

Lord, I don't want this fast to just go by with me on autopilot ... just wishing and waiting for it to be done. I want to dig in with You, learning to push in hard, and touching You with every part of me. I want to go deep and high into the depth of You ... into Your love, into a high revelation with You. I want a new deepness. I want a deep forging of my spirit.

It's weird, Lord. As hard as fasting is, I would be disappointed if I was released from it tomorrow. (I am feeling ice—Holy Spirit—in my veins.)

Lord, show me what my fast is doing ... share with me its purpose. I know I may not truly understand this side of Heaven, but I have to trust that I do it because You told me to ...

The Ancient Path

It is showing your heart for Me. Like Abraham, you put nothing in front of Me. You hold nothing back.

DAY 15

Felt like today was a fast day for healing for the list of people You gave me. This day was not too difficult; hunger abated mostly—pockets only.

Lord, I had such a sweet time in Your presence two nights ago, laying in such incredible peace, with Holy Spirit blowing on my face. I am feeling so grateful for chicken soup smell, a warm bed and house, a vehicle that works, for my parents, family, kids, friends, job. Lord, I have so much.

Such deep peace comes over me when I lay in Your presence during this fast. I believe You are taking me to deeper levels of trust and faith. You, who can move mountains, love to fellowship with me intimately. How much more can You do to move the mountains in my life. In quietness and confidence is your strength. In quietness and confidence is _my_ strength.

"Don't underestimate rest and peace. It is a powerful weapon, resting in My peace. It sustains you, draws others unto Me, enlightens others, teaches others. I am healing your body inside out. I am drawing you unto Me, unto My power. I am strengthening every part of you, your mind, your body, your spirit. Everything is being sharpened. There is much ahead of you that must be accomplished. You must be fully prepared, fully put on the altar, every part of you. I am drawing the poison out of you, to your very depths. Let it go. You will see clearly. You will smell. You will taste. I heal all your diseases. I bring peace to your body. Yes, feel it even now. I am teaching you about having a healthy body, mind, and spirit."

It is so hard to believe I can still function after 17 days of not eating ... I'm not dizzy or light-headed or woozy. You are sustaining me, Lord!
"I will sustain you if you trust Me. "

"Frame your day with Me."

DAY 19

Hunger pains ...
The first few days of the fast my tummy cried out in hunger pains. As the days went past, as my body was deprived of food, it quit crying out. It's the same with other lusts of the flesh ... your craving and physical needing of it goes away—surrendered ...

The Ancient Path

DAY 22

I look back and I had this monumental fast ahead of me that I didn't know how I was going to get through ... Now I have 9 days left. I am over 2/3 done. The Lord really does sustain. The physical pains have long gone and not returned other than slight pockets of a bit of rawness. The mental battle is the hardest. I can't look forward and think, "A week from now I still won't have eaten ..." That kind of thinking leads to discouragement. I need to think, "Am I okay right now? Yes. I am okay right now and that is all I need to see." God gives you grace for the moment ... His mercies are new every morning. I am starting to understand that better. It has been long and grueling to some degree ... yet not really. The aspect of warfare has been ... rest in His peace!! Maybe more direct warfare will come, but right now it is being sustained in a state of Sweet Peace and rest of the Lord!

"Be at peace, My child. Drink in My peace. Drink in My stillness. My breath breathes on you. My breath is in you. It surrounds you, giving you peace, and keeping the battle that rages, far from your heart. In the stillness is My wisdom. In My breath is Power. Power comes to you, child. Surge forward; pieces of the puzzle have been placed. Have confidence in this, child, You did well. The end draws near, but it is just the beginning. Fear dissipates as you draw close to Me. Fear dissipates as you walk with Me. I have set your path. Do not be afraid to take it. Draw your heart close."

The Ancient Path

[Received prayer from three friends on separate occasions.]

DAY 26

The fast is hard. I am getting quite thin, wondering how I will be sustained 5 more days ... but God will sustain. My friend said Jesus was holding my right hand. He was leading, but by my side. My other friend gave me Psalm 37: "The Lord directs the steps of the godly. He delights in every detail of their lives. Though they stumble, they will never fall, for the Lord holds them by the hand ..."
Lord, on these last 5 days of the fast, I don't want to wish them away or pray they go by fast; I want to get every bit of mileage out of them I can. I want to soak deep in Your presence and languish in Your love and always remember them with a sweet fondness of how close I felt to You ... Lord, I draw near to You over these days. Order my days, my time, my minutes. Let them be pleasing to both of us.

"I go with you. You are doing everything as I ask, My child. Peace be still. Though the battle rages around you, you are safe in the palm of My hand. Do not fear. It will accomplish all as I have set it out. The pit of hell wages war against you, but the battle is Mine. Guard your mind. That is where he will attack. He tries to bring unrest, to erode your confident trust in Me. Trust is crucial where we are going—absolute, infallible trust in My leading ... Do not let sorrow close to your heart. I bring forth joy. I release deep joy in your life—so much joy. My promises are true. Cling to them. Grow your faith. Grow your trust. You are being tested to ensure you are made of steel and diamonds, as a sword, and just as sharp.

I smile over you! I am excited about all I have in store for you! Get excited! Be abandoned to all I call you to! Have no fear! Rush in! Let it carry you! The tides will turn and carry you out to the ocean beyond all you can imagine. You will be so far in over your head; it will be marvelous!"

[I chose the last day of the fast as my celebration day, rather than the day I was finished. Not sure why. Seemed important.]

DAY 30

Lord, today, You and I celebrate! Please send Your angels to minister to me at the end of this last fast day! Lord, I so appreciate and am grateful for all You have given me. I know I have to live more in the moment, not always looking ahead. I trust You to sustain me in all areas. I give You back all the promises You have given me and I lay them down on Isaac's altar. Lord, You have carried me through this fast! Make me Your glory! Make me like You!

Journal Entry Excerpts - January , 2017 [The day after the fast]:

Lord, we did it! Thirty days of self denying ... not eating! Seemed impossible. It was long and hard, but You sustained me. I feel deeper peace and trust. I am so much more grateful for the things I have and can do, and for my health.

Isaiah 30:15b (NLT)
In quietness and confidence is your strength.

Exodus 14:13
… "Don't be afraid. Just stand still and watch the LORD rescue you today."…

Psalm 46:10
Be still, and know that I am God …

Wow Lord! Calm.

Peace.

Absolute trust.

Be still

Watch & wait in full confidence ... I know what I need to do ...

The Ancient Path

Message received ... the theme of my fast, perfectly summed up in Your Scripture [for] today. I will watch and wait ...

There are times when I have been released early from fasts. It was during those times when I had believed I was to cover another for a specified time frame, such as the duration of their mission trip, but once an impartation was given, a major step of faith taken, or a time of prayer had, though the initial number of days had not yet passed, I recognized that had been *my* time frame—not *His* time frame and in fulfillment of *His purpose*—and I was immediately released from the fast.

All throughout this fast, however, even when I had felt I couldn't possibly keep going, I knew deep in my soul that I could not bow out. The fast had to be brought to full completion; the Lord had made it quite clear that quitting was *not* an option. It was one of those experiences where you are extremely grateful to have done it —but not overly enthusiastic at the prospect of having to do it again. It had been *hard,* and physically painful. This made my heart conflict when, towards the latter part of the thirty days, He started preparing me—the year would not be out and I would be called to fast again, and this time, for forty days. I tried my hand at bargaining: "Could I just tack on ten more days now instead?" came my feeble attempt to short-circuit the work the Lord wanted to do in me.

The Ancient Path

Seven months later, the Lord again began to stir the fasting waters. Videos and Scriptures began the summons. Walking into church one fall morning, I conferred with my friend, "I think the Lord wants me to do my forty day fast now ... and I think I have to borrow a juicer for it!"

It was no surprise when she gave me an incredulous look and announced that just yesterday, her son had pulled out his juicer, after years of storage, to photograph it, wanting to put it up for sale. I'll admit, I cried (just a bit) after it had been confirmed. As amazing as my extended fast experience had been, I was not yet ready to visit it again so very soon. But once again, it was not an option—unless I chose to be disobedient.

"Devouring" Scripture was my directive in conjunction with this fast. The Lord required me to read through the Bible as I fasted the forty days, then continue on at a pace to work through it within a six month time-period or less. [On a side note, once I read through Genesis, the Lord said, "Read it again, and this time with a commentary. My wide-eyed response was, "Lord, how am I supposed to get through the Bible in six months if I have to read everything twice?" His laughing response that came to my spirit was, "You do not have to read everything twice, just Genesis. A solid understanding of Genesis is necessary to understand the rest of Scripture." Borrowing a commentary for the Book of Genesis, I turned to the introductory pages, and there, highlighted in yellow, was the exact phrase the Lord had told me, almost word for word.

Despite the daunting 600 pages of the book, given the tight timeline, I knew it was the right one, and that I had heard correctly.]

This *devouring of Scripture* became my food during the fast—from day one, I never had a single intense hunger pain throughout the entire forty days. Though I still had to fight the mental battle, the physical one was covered by His grace. I believe part of my testing within this second extended fast was, *Would I be obedient*, knowing how hard the first one was—not knowing He would so radically pull me through it …

The shift from this time of fasting in my life has been incredible. I learned to strengthen myself in the Lord through prayer (both with understanding and in the spirit), praise, worship, and gratefulness. My hearing of His voice intensified, making following the mystery of His divine guidance that much easier. I sensed detailed things, knew strategies of the enemy, and how to counteract them. The level of trust between the Lord and I was taken to an inconceivable new depth. I learned to live in the moment, knowing He will give me the grace to "do today," and tomorrow He will give me the grace to do that day. That alone changes you. Life is not wasted waiting for the next hour, the next day, the next weekend, the next *thing*. Anxiety of what is to come, what may come, does not exist when you live in the moment; you simply trust He will take you through everything on your path, and give You everything you need, as you need it. And considering the difficult path I often find myself on, I am thankful for this hard lesson.

The Ancient Path

Let's pray for the continued hard lessons I know the Lord wants to take us all through.

Dear Heavenly Father,
I willingly put my life into Your hands of mercy and grace. Through Your hands of mercy, peace washes over me. You answer me when I call from the depths, pulling me out of the pit. Through Your hands of grace, I will be refined and defined. And that sometimes is not comfortable.

I repent for every time You have asked something of me which I ignored or willfully chose not to do. I want to be realigned with Your Word of who I am in You, with Christ living in me—my identity in You—and that takes hard work: mentally, emotionally, physically, and spiritually. Lord, grant me the tenacity, fortitude, strength, and courage I need, to do what it takes to become a sanctified, purified vessel fit for Your service—to become who You originally designed me to be.

Help me change my language so it aligns with Your plans, Your words over me, instead of lies of the enemy, and the faulty, distorted perspective of the world. Let not my own selfish desires or lack of discipline trump my obedience to You and the refining work You desire me to endure. Let me walk willingly into the fire You have created for me, and stay there until the exact hour You have deemed as acceptable. Show me what that is and how to do it. Lead me to the wisdom, knowledge, information, and other resources I need to make this possible. Bring the people I need beside me into my life, so I may walk this path with other like-minded people on a similar journey of ascension.

Grant unto me the strength and determination I need to let go of my own agenda, stop trying to figure it out and do it on my own, and grasp fully onto the plans You have for me—they are so much higher than my own, and You know the depth I need developed in my life to carry out all You have designated to be on my path. Take me on Your ancient path, so I may walk the present path You have laid out for me. I ask this all in the name of Jesus, my strength. Amen.

I will bring the *one*-third through the fire, Will refine them as silver is refined, And test them as gold is tested. They will call on My name, And I will answer them. I will say, 'This *is* My people'; And each one will say, 'The LORD *is* my God.'"
Zechariah 13:9

For I have bent Judah, My bow, Fitted the bow with Ephraim, And raised up your sons, O Zion, Against your sons, O Greece, And made you like the sword of a mighty man.
Zechariah 9:13

The Ancient Path

Connect the Dots:

_____

_____

_____

_____

_____

_____

_____

_____

_____

_____

_____

_____

_____

_____

_____

_____

_____

22. IN THE QUIET

But let him ask in faith, with no doubting, for he who doubts is like a wave of the sea driven and tossed by the wind. For let not that man suppose that he will receive anything from the Lord; *he is* a double-minded man, unstable in all his ways.

James 1:6-8

Strategy to Implement

Remain unmoved and ever faithful, even more so in the quiet times.

I love the times and seasons of His rain. This is when the Lord gives me pages upon pages of revelation as the words pour out of my pen within the margins of my journal; words both for me and for others. I treasure the wisdom, encouragement, and love the Savior pours out on the lines of the little white pages. It is also during these times that I marvel at the strong sense of direction placed deep within my spirit. My path is clearly defined—I know precisely where to go, when to go, what to do, to whom I should speak, and what I am to pray. I am able to step out boldly and confidently in all He asks of me. I feel so close and connected to Him, overwhelmed by the flow of intimacy. And it is these very times that make the other times, the quiet times, so excruciating—almost unbearable.

In these times, the quiet times, each word of revelation is hard fought; a battle raged marks every step taken. Questions of, "What am I doing wrong, Lord? Why am I not hearing Your voice? Are You still there? What do I do?" arise unceasingly. Our vision becomes murky, our path fuzzy, and we may begin to believe we are drifting aimlessly. The feelings of being forsaken, left, abandoned,

The Ancient Path

can begin to shake our faith, making us doubtful and double-minded. We can begin to question whether God cares about, or loves us. We may even begin to question His very existence.

Though walking in His ways at times may be a hardship, *determining* them is not difficult when He speaks to us with the voice of thunder. It is another matter entirely when it is the barely-discernible whisper that seeks to guide our steps. When we first begin our walk in His ways or when we do not spend time listening at His feet, His voice often appears faint and far off. But once we have become accustomed to the precision and clarity of His booming voice, our plight becomes painful when His voice seemingly fades away.

It is in these moments, in these seasons, when we can let ourselves become adrift like a lifeboat lost at sea, or we can press in, choosing to believe His Word and promise that He will not leave nor forsake us, no matter our circumstances, present experience, or earthly perspective. This is when the true testing begins. Will we still remain faithful and obedient when those words of encouragement, words of direction, seem to be caught up in the heavenlies rather than making it down into our spirits? Will we do what it takes to press in and obtain, and then treasure each scarce nugget that has struggled through the oppressive atmosphere? Will we trust that He still has plans for us when we seem all but forgotten? Will we do what it takes to press in harder and harder, and continue to follow through on the last set of instructions we were given, without any fresh words?

And greater still, will we be able to rest in the assurances of Scripture, believing them far above our present circumstances? Will we be able to prophesy His promises in faith and belief, speaking into existence the things that are not? Or will we turn to talk of doubt and pessimism, empowering the enemy with our negative words? Will we remain steadfast, unwavering in the quiet? Or will we be tossed about, becoming double-minded and unstable? Will we be able to keep grasping on to the hope that keeps us afloat, no matter how long we have already been holding on? Will we be determined to keep strengthening ourselves in the Lord rather than giving in to the depression that taunts us, even when all seems lost and we have nothing left? Will we be able to praise Him while doing so?

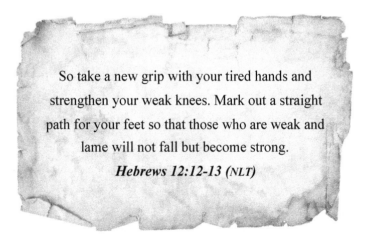

So take a new grip with your tired hands and strengthen your weak knees. Mark out a straight path for your feet so that those who are weak and lame will not fall but become strong.

Hebrews 12:12-13 (NLT)

The Ancient Path

I have experienced quiet times when the Lord had told me what to do, and He does not tell me anything further until I have done all He had asked of me. In other words, He already told me what He had to tell me, and there is nothing more to say until I have completed what He had told me. This can be one source of the quiet. It is then up to me to follow through on what He had mandated for me. Only as I near completion will He give me anything further, not wanting, I believe, to overwhelm me with too many projects, directions, and tasks at once.

Other times, my own sin can prevent me from hearing from the Lord. We can create a barrier against the Lord's voice when we have an attitude or fear of Him addressing something we don't particularly want to hear; at least not at the moment. We harden our hearts and sear our consciences, inviting in an attitude of rebellion. It is during these times I need to do my part, which is to repent. Even our woundings can keep us from hearing from the Lord and can distort His voice, causing us to see through such filters as rejection, anger, or bitterness. It is then we need to seek others to lead us in our healing.

At one time in my life, I felt like I was in a big, black, concrete box, and all my prayers ruthlessly bounced off the ceiling back at me. It was then I was reliant on the voice of others to hear God for me, and help me heal enough so I could seek Him and hear from Him on my own.

The Ancient Path

In other times of quiet, the Lord can be calling us to a new way to hear Him. In our desperate search for His voice, we do just that— search—opening up new modes of communication available to us we didn't know existed—hadn't bothered to seek out before; did not have the need. The quiet can simply be this invitation to explore. We can become dependent on "*the way* in which we hear God," and mistakenly believe that is the *only* way the Lord can speak to us (and we sometimes extend that limitation onto other people). In these seasons, we are encouraged to hone and sharpen perhaps less *used,* less *trusted* ways of hearing Him, so we trust them as much as the ways in which we are used to hearing His voice. Like a well-armed soldier, we need many weapons in our arsenal so we can be ready at a moment's notice for any and every situation.

Prophetic word - May 2017 (abridged)

You'd like God to come to you the same way all the time. It's like when they keep taking horses through a drill with all kinds of scary scenarios so the horse will trust the owner and the owner will know the horse. It is that kind of process. God is leading you through these scary kinds of things, but every time He leads you through, the trust is building and you are getting to the place where … "Ok, He's leading, I know I can trust Him; I am going with Him." You wish He'd do it the same way all the time so you'd know it was Him, but He is walking you through this process where you can trust Him with this childlike innocence. Wherever He leads, wherever you go together you know, you know, you know He's got your back, He's got your front, He is that wall of protection you've always wanted and needed and wished you'd had.

— Maryanne Ward

As frustrating as my recent quiet season was, I grew to realize I could trust what I sensed in the spirit as much as I could trust what I physically saw; and what I sensed to do, I could trust as much as when the Lord gave me downloads of directives through the words flowing out of my pen. On the battlefield, when the fight is fierce, the Lord has to trust me with instantly hearing and doing exactly what He commands—lives could depend on it. I may not always have the luxury of stopping and pulling out my pen or asking seventeen other people for confirming words ...

Much can be learned in a season of quiet, but sometimes it is not a season of learning at all, but rather, a silent command to rest. The Lord is asking us to put down our sword and take the time to heal and recover from whatever we have been through, or rest in preparation for the taxing season on the path just up ahead.

Many times after engaging in spiritual warfare, I am mentally exhausted and physically sore. (Warfare is not to be taken lightly.) I have been told I have many battle scars. Scars are healed wounds. They were all bleeding at one point, and with each new gash, rest and time in His presence, whether He is speaking or just silently attending to us, is required to properly cleanse, heal, and seal the wound, without which, leads to ugly spiritual infections.

After my recent Healing Identity seminar, I took the time to dine with the Lord Jesus. (I poured Him His own cup of sparkling juice.) Lying quietly beside the crackling fire, I sensed that Jesus, the Commander of the Heavenly Army, had sent His angels to minister to me after the warfare of the weekend. They were gently putting flower petals over each one of my wounds.

It is in these precious times, while we are quiet before Him, all around us is quiet, that He can heal and refill us, so we continue to move forth in His strength, rather than our own. He will not give us any new assignments while we are still gushing blood. And we need to be at peace with doing *nothing*, when that is what exactly what the Lord requests us to do—for as long as He says to do it. Rather than fighting a quiet time of rest, embrace it. Know that even when He *seems* far away, you can trust that He is still right by your side, walking with You along the path, perhaps even carrying you. Come, let's pray…

The Ancient Path

Dear Lord,

Thank you for the quiet time. Thank you for being the friend by my side, with whom I know all is well, whether we are eagerly engaged in conversation, or quietly walking along together. Your Word says You will never abandon me, forsake me, or leave me. I trust in Your Word. Help me align with it no matter the season I am in. Let me stand solid in my faith, unmoved and ever faithful in the quiet times, never questioning Your faithfulness or goodness. I ask for the determination and the courage I need to press in harder when I need to do so.

If I have unfulfilled requirements You are quietly waiting for me to complete so we can continue to move forward together, please bring them to mind. Help me build the endurance and perseverance I need to always be faithful in finishing what You ask of me.

Lord, if I have any unexamined areas in my life, or any areas where I have labeled "Do not touch," please help me allow You to shine Your light on them, exposing them for what they are, so I can deal with them. I do not want any barriers between me and Thee. Lord, You make me brave. Make me brave!

Grant unto me the strength I need to walk through the pain that leads to healing. Let me always do what it takes to surrender these areas unto You. Keep the soil of my heart soft and my conscience open to Your voice. I repent of any doubt that has crept in during the times of silence. I shall be stable in all my ways, standing strong against any wind. I bind up the spirit of rebellion; I refuse to partner with enemy lies and shame which try to keep me silent. Please bring others onto my path to help steady me when I have stumbled, and get up when I have fallen.

Please expose any bitterness or anger I have allowed to take root in my heart and remove any filters which distort Your voice and the wisdom given to me by the wise counsel You have put in my life.

Lord, when my quiet times are to stretch and grow me in accessing Your voice differently, keep me open to Your training. I surrender myself to Your sharpening instruments. Let me be faithful in the training, so I can become the well-armed, elite warrior You are calling me to be.

Lord, every time you require me to put down my sword and rest, heal, recover, or prepare, let me be faithful in not questioning You. I bind up any guilt that says I need to push through when You have told me to rest. Let me see Your rest like a chamber of peace, wrapping around my body, soul, and spirit, filling me with all I need to be ready when you once again call me forth from the shadows and onto the battlefield. Let me learn to treasure the quiet times, knowing that you are still faithfully by my side, and will always be. I pray this in the powerful name of Jesus Christ, my Savior.

The Ancient Path

Connect the Dots:

_____

_____

_____

_____

_____

_____

_____

_____

_____

_____

_____

_____

_____

_____

_____

_____

And the word of the LORD came to me,
saying, "Jeremiah, what do you see?"
And I said, "I see an almond branch."
Then the LORD said to me, "You see
well, for I am watching over my word
to perform it."

Jeremiah 1:11-12 (ESV)

Strategy to Implement

Prophetic words are blueprints for your journey. Transcribe them. Read them often. Pray into them, declare out of them, and act upon them. (Just don't try to make them happen or put a timeline on them!)

Though it was one of the shortest words of prophecy spoken over me—only one sentence—it has been one of the most profound to date: "I see you with a saber, and you are cutting through the veil like Zoro."

For many months after receiving that word, my mind kept returning to the thought of a sword. In my mind, it was a short bladed one—more like a dagger. For some reason it was significant. After some exploration, the sense arose that perhaps the Lord wanted me to have one in the physical. Thinking that a bit on the *odd* side, I shelved the thought once more. But it persisted.

Walking through the mall shortly thereafter, I conceded to at least consider it was actually a directive from the Lord, as strange as it was. *If I see a dagger in the knife shop and I absolutely know it is the right one, I'll buy it for myself as my birthday present.* Half thinking I was crazy, yet a little intrigued with the idea, I scrutinized the knives and small swords in the display case. I had only recently been healed of an irrational fear of knives, making my actions seem even more out of character for me. At the time, I didn't really believe I would find *the one*. Yet two-thirds of the way around the u-shaped case, there it was. My dagger. I knew it instantly. It had an ornate rosewood handle and was made with Damascus steel. I didn't even know what Damascus steel was, but later found out it was historically forged at high temperatures and made by folding layer upon layer of steel back upon itself, pushing it past its breaking point time and again. The result was a strong blade resistant to shattering that would keep its sharp edge. That in itself was highly symbolic and reflective of my journey.

Stunned, I walked straight out of the shop. *If I still feel I should literally buy myself this dagger for my birthday by the time I have finished my other errands in the mall ... I'll go back and buy it,* I bargained with myself. I am not sure if I was trying to talk myself *out of* or *into* buying it. Deep in my spirit, however, I knew there was no way I'd be leaving the mall without it. It had been made for me. Literally.

For the next couple of weeks, the dagger sat in its sheath on the high shelf in my closet. I was not totally comfortable with the idea of having it in my house. That all changed, however, with the words given to me by friends several weeks later at my birthday celebration.

Prophetic Word - March 2017 (abridged)

I saw that you had picked up that dagger. I feel like the Lord says, "I'm going to teach you how to wield it. It is not hard because it won't be *you* wielding it. I'll be having your hand in My hand. But I can't pick it up. You've got to pick it up then wait until I pick your hand up, and I'll teach you."

God wants you to pick up that sword and start slicing through the air. By doing that you are going be entering and piercing into the spiritual realm. Don't wait for Him to tell you when to do it. He is telling you now; this is His voice saying, "Pick it up, every time you have a chance, every opportunity you get, pick it up, hold it tight, even if you don't know what you are doing. I know what I am doing. Thrust it into the air and I will make sure you are accurate and I will put the blade where it needs to be. Even though you can't see what you are hitting, I can see what you are hitting."

You know that movie Karate Kid where the guy does *wax on* and *wax off*? That is what you have been doing all this time. All these things you have been doing in the spirit and that you have been doing symbolically have been *wax on, wax off*. All that time you have been learning what you need to know so when you step into that ring, which for you is picking up that sword, everything you have learned is going to come into play and suddenly it is all going to make sense and suddenly you are going to know what you are doing and suddenly you are going to have an awareness and this power and this understanding. You are going to defeat enemies, whether you see them or not, you are going to defeat enemies.

— Kimm Reid

A long time ago the Lord told you, "You are a warrior woman." Actually, in a sense you have been wielding a dagger, but a spiritual one. This is the physical dagger that you now have and God is going to teach you how to use that. I hear the word "accurate." You are going to become really accurate with that sword.

— Pixie Hoffman

These timely prophetic words from my friends on my birthday more than confirmed the words I had heard from the Lord the previous night: "Pick up your sword and learn how to use it. Wield it well. Wield it often." Those words reassured me that though *this whole thing seemed crazy … I … actually … wasn't!*

Since then, the Lord has asked me to wield the dagger many times during warfare. I trust Him to put the blade where it needs to be. I have noticed that my prayer language (tongues) are different when I have the dagger in my hands, and I believe things have been accomplished and victories won that would not have come without it in my hands—perhaps even battles of life and death. My friend graciously opens her journal to share one such battle with you [interspersed with my commentary].

Monday, July 9, 2018

Resting was over and I had a paint job. Left home happy, but within an hour, something odd came over me and I seemed unable to fight it. I knew the enemy was attacking my mind, but I didn't care. I told myself to turn on worship to battle my thoughts, to speak truth, all the things I knew to do, yet I did nothing. It wasn't that I "couldn't," rather that I didn't want to. It felt as though my soul had died or something, which I can't explain. The thoughts in my head were not ones of suicide, but rather of letting go of life. I knew the enemy was encouraging me to just give myself over to him and I would not wake up the next morning. It would all be over.

I finished the job and went home with my soul dead. It was as though something —the thing that gives life—had left me and only my shell of a body remained walking aimlessly, driving home aimlessly. Hard to explain. I kept hearing the enemy tell me how to go to sleep—how to fall asleep—with my arms crossed over my chest—and say one sentence before going to sleep: "Take me, I'm done." It was not that I could fight it; it wasn't that I heard taunting, like usual, just a knowing that was what I would do. I wrote in my journal, "July 9, I got nothing left, I'm done."

Jocelyn texted an hour later to see if we could pray and I said, "I guess." She wasn't calling about me, and when she called, I said, "I'm not going to pray, but I'll listen to you." I saw myself in front of me, and my skin slipped off and fell to the floor. I watched myself die, I believe. My soul was being removed from my body. Jos prayed for a moment and then began praying for me ...

[As soon as I had started talking to Kimm, I knew something was desperately wrong. This was not her; I had no idea who this person on the phone was, but it was not my friend—not anyone even remotely whom I knew my good friend to be. I began to pray for her. I heard the words "Ice man" in my spirit. It made sense. It was like she had been taken over by a cold, detached personality, void of all life and any vitality.]

Later she said I sounded dead—lifeless. She prayed against "The ice man." As she did, I saw a leviathan rise up and begin to scream. The more Jos prayed, the more ferociously the leviathan thrashed and the more it screamed. I told Jos she was making an impact. [She also told me it was annoying him, only succeeding in making him madder.] She said, "Hold on." I still didn't care.

[As she was describing this scene to me I was horrified, but it didn't even seem to matter to her what was happening or what would happen in the end. It really did seem like she was already dead. This was not my friend with whom I had faced so many battles, my friend whom I would choose over any other to fight by my side. This scared me. I knew I was to get my dagger. This spirit, this dragon attacking my friend, had to be slain. Her life seemed to depend on it.]

The Ancient Path

She came back soon with her dagger and I could hear her praying and swinging her dagger. As she did, the leviathan screamed louder and thrashed harder, as though the dagger was literally hitting it. I told her what I was seeing and finally, she gave one last stabbing (I saw in the spirit her standing beneath the beast as it rose high above her and thrashed and screamed—I saw her stab it in the underbelly) and I heard the beast shriek as his last breath was leaving him and he slumped down, dead. [I am actually glad I saw none of this.]

I physically felt a release and I was back. I said, "It's dead," and Jos said, "YOU'RE BACK!" [In the two words Kimm spoke, I knew *instantly* it was her. She was herself again. She had returned from wherever she had gone. Overwhelming relief flooded over me as my friend had returned as if from the grave. I had never experienced anything like it.]

And I was. I knew I'd beaten death and we had the victory. I began jumping and screaming, saying, "We won! We beat you! We beat death!"

—Kimm Reid

I am ever so thankful I had acted upon that simple prophetic word given to me. We may never truly understand the drastic importance of following the instruction of the Lord—His blueprints. He gives us these words for a reason. Everything in His game plan is strategic. Everything is for a purpose. Study His words to you. Know them. Put them into action. How many things have we missed because we did not take it seriously enough? How many battles have been lost because we didn't do our part? Yes, test them, making sure they line up with Scripture (1 Thessalonians 5:21, 1 John 4:1), but then don't put them on the shelf, assuming they are for later, without praying into them. He always does His part, and He will make your part known to you as you seek Him and learn to follow His leading. Heed His word, I implore you. Your life, or that of someone you love, may depend on it.

Welcome to spiritual warfare.
Draw Your Sword ...

Dear Lord of Angel Armies,
I stand before You, ready and willing to do Your bidding. Make me able. Take my hand in Yours, and lead me. Remind me of all the words You have spoken over me, and show me how to engage with them. I know I cannot bring them to pass—dare not bring them to pass—but I know I have a part to play in preparation for them. Show me what to do! My life is literally in Your hands, and I know no better place for it to be. Raise me up. Let me step up higher. Take me on the ancient path of ascension, making me more like You. Reveal to me the strategic plans You have for my life; I do not want to miss even one thing because of lack on my part. Help me heed Your word, always.

Guard my heart and mind from false prophecies, curses, and negative words spoken over me. I break those off my life and the lives of my family and friends. Increase my discernment so I know what is from You and what is meant for evil or distraction. Fill my heart and mind with Your words to me, who I am in You—my identity—and lead me to speak that over myself and others. Through Your words to me, light a flame and keep it burning—consume me with Your holy fire, bringing me closer and closer to Your likeness, that my life may be a living sacrifice, pleasing to You, and acceptable in Your sight.

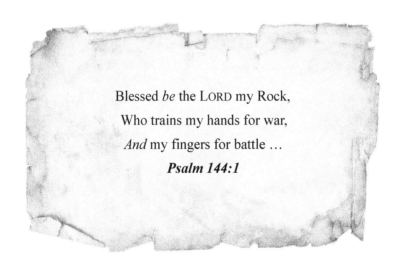

Blessed *be* the LORD my Rock,
Who trains my hands for war,
And my fingers for battle …
Psalm 144:1

Connect the Dots:

_____

_____

_____

_____

_____

_____

_____

_____

_____

_____

_____

_____

_____

_____

_____

_____

_____

A FINAL WORD

Now the LORD spoke to Moses
and Aaron in the
land of Egypt, saying:
"This month *shall be* your
beginning of months;
it *shall be* the first month of the
year to you.
Exodus 12:1-2

The Ancient Path

So it was, after three days, that the officers went through the camp; and they commanded the people, saying, "When you see the ark of the covenant of the LORD your God, and the priests, the Levites, bearing it, then you shall set out from your place and go after it.

"Yet there shall be a space between you and it, about two thousand cubits by measure. Do not come near it, that you may know the way by which you must go, for you have not passed *this* way before."

And Joshua said to the people, "Sanctify yourselves, for tomorrow the LORD will do wonders among you."

… and as those who bore the ark came to the Jordan, and the feet of the priests who bore the ark dipped in the edge of the water (for the Jordan overflows all its bank during the whole time of harvest), that the waters stood still, and rose in a heap very far away at Adam, the city that is beside Zaretan. So the waters that went down into the Sea of the Arabah, the Salt Sea, failed, and were cut off; and the people crossed over opposite Jericho.

Then the priests who bore the ark of the covenant of the LORD stood firm on dry ground in the midst of the Jordan; and all Israel crossed over on dry ground, until all the people had crossed completely over the Jordan.

Joshua 3:2-5, 15-17

The Ancient Path

Prophetic word - October 2018

This might be the same word I gave you last time … many feet have travelled that path but only few have actually crossed it. I feel this is something the Lord wants to ingrain in you that many have tried to cross this path but many have failed. But He is going to give you the way to … get across …

—Glen Paguyo

Lord, the book is called "The Ancient Path." Why are the cover and bookends (front and back Scripture verses) focused on memorial stones? What does a pathway have to do with …. Oh … Crossing the Jordan <u>was the Israelites' miraculous pathway</u> into the Promised Land. That was the walk of faith You had designed for them. What began with the Lord's instructions to Moses and Aaron at Passover ended at the Jordan with Joshua. As they crossed the mighty river on dry ground—at the end of their ancient path—the Lord was ushering them into a new era.

Invariably, the Father takes me through the very things He intends for me to write. I was finished my season in the crucible. I was also done "sitting in the hallway"—waiting in my time of transition. I was now crossing over into the Promised Land. Only I didn't have to cross a river bed—I simply had to close one journal and open the next; very fitting for me! A month or so previously, the Lord had sent me to buy a new journal. Feeling it was to be a significant one, I upped the ante and went to a higher-end store than my regular dollar-store-variety. Four journals caught my eye. For "some odd reason" I put the one I liked the best back on the shelf. My second favorite was also re-shelved, to be later suggested to someone over whom I would prophesy. I was left with a soft pink one that read "HEY LOVELY," and a sky blue one (think back to the beginning of this book and you'll know where this is going…) with the words: "THE SKY'S THE LIMIT." I hadn't wanted to buy even one, and now I had to buy two.

However, I knew deep in my spirit that when I finished the last page of the pink one, and again picked up my pen to write, this time in the blue one, a significant shift would have occurred. What I didn't know was that even the date would be poignantly significant. Within a week I was already seeing evidence of this spiritual shift. I was able to hold my first Healing Identity Seminar in the exact format the Lord had shown me. I did not have to choose between buying milk or deodorant for my teen. The Lord restored my career —*double*—returning me to the place I considered *home*. And new opportunities presented themselves.

[On a side note, I had previously run a pilot session for my seminar, but the format was different and the cover of the book had since changed—which is a story in itself. And at the seminar, I started the morning with tea, in a cup provided by the lovely bed and breakfast venue. Note the words on the teacup! I also received a birthday card that day, signed by all the seminar participants. The words on the card echoed the words of the sky blue journal. You can't help but feel cared for when the Lord God, creator of the heavens, attends to such detail, all to reassure me and speak to my heart!]

I had reached the end of a long, hard, almost unbearable stage of my journey—through the storm, through the fire, and in water way over my head. I was finally able to step off the precipice (for now) —I had crossed the ancient path. He had given me the way.

Journal Entry - March 2019

Receive My love, child. Receive My blessing. All will be done as I have said. It will come fast now. You have stood through the fire and passed the tests. All will be well for you and your family. Blessings will rain down upon you and your tribe.

So the LORD said to Moses, "I will also do this thing that you have spoken; for you have found grace in My sight, and I know you by name (Exodus 33:17).

[The last line in my pink, HEY LOVELY Journal]
And with this I close the book on an era ... an era of fire, flood, famine ... where You grew my courage and strength and taught me to breathe underwater ...

Let's pray Psalm 145 from the Holy Scriptures as you continue on your path, finding the ancient one on which He wants you to tread, *for you have not passed this way before*. Let a new era begin …

The Ancient Path

I will extol You, my God, O King;
And I will bless Your name forever and ever.
Every day I will bless You,
And I will praise Your name forever and ever.
Great *is* the LORD, and greatly to be praised;
And His greatness *is* unsearchable.

One generation shall praise Your works to another,
And shall declare Your mighty acts.
I will meditate on the glorious splendor of Your majesty,
And on Your wondrous works.
Men shall speak of the might of Your awesome acts,
And I will declare Your greatness.
They shall utter the memory of Your great goodness,
And shall sing of Your righteousness.

The LORD *is* gracious and full of compassion,
Slow to anger and great in mercy.
The LORD *is* good to all,
And His tender mercies are over all His works.

All Your works shall praise You, O LORD,
And Your saints shall bless You.
They shall speak of the glory of Your kingdom,

The Ancient Path

And talk of Your power,
To make known to the sons of men His mighty acts,
And the glorious majesty of His kingdom.
Your kingdom *is* an everlasting kingdom,
And Your dominion *endures* throughout all generations.

The LORD upholds all who fall,
And raises up all *who are* bowed down.
The eyes of all look expectantly to You,
And You give them their food in due season.
You open Your hand
And satisfy the desire of every living thing.

The LORD *is* righteous in all His ways,
Gracious in all His works.
The Lord *is* near to all who call upon Him,
To all who call upon Him in truth.
He will fulfill the desire of those who fear Him;
He will also hear their cry and save them.
The Lord preserves all who love Him,
But all the wicked He will destroy.
My mouth shall speak the praise of the Lord,
And all flesh shall bless His holy name
Forever and ever.

Then he spoke to the children of Israel, saying: "When your children ask their fathers in time to come, saying, 'What *are* these stones?' **22** then you shall let your children know, saying, 'Israel crossed over this Jordan on dry land'; **23** for the Lord your God dried up the waters of the Jordan before you until you had crossed over, as the Lord your God did to the Red Sea, which He dried up before us until we had crossed over, **24** that all the peoples of the earth may know the hand of the Lord, that it *is* mighty, that you may fear the Lord your God forever."

Joshua 4:21-24

Endnotes

1 Carol Nemitz, Collection of Prophetic Meanings of Colors by Carol Nemitz - Facebook. https://m.facebook.com. Accessed October 13, 2018.

2 Cooke, Graham. *The Way of the Warrior.* Brilliant Book House, 2008, CD.

3 Healy, Blake. *The Veil: An Invitation to the Unseen Realm.* Lake Mary: Charisma House, 2018.

4 Byrd, Ian. *Life is a Highway: A Roadmap for Your Journey.* Calgary: Forerunner Press, 2018.

5 Drozda, Jocelyn. *Invisible No More: Answering the Call to Arms.* Helena: Ahelia Publishing, Inc, 2018.

6 Blown Away. YouTube. 4:41. carrieunderwoodVEVO, August 1, 2012.

7 Drozda, Jocelyn. *Invisible No More: Answering the Call to Arms. Book III: Aligning with Destiny.*
    Helena: Ahelia Publishing, Inc, (TBA).

8 Reid, Kimm. *Casting Shadows: Beyond Solstice Gates. Helena: Ahelia Publishing, Inc, 2015.*

9 Drozda, Jocelyn. *Invisible No More: Answering the Call to Arms. Book II: Personal Identity Restored.*
    Helena: Ahelia Publishing, Inc, 2018.

Summary of Strategies to Implement

✔ Choose the narrow gate and open yourself up to walking in His ways.

✔ Ask the Lord for a sign. He wants to lead you into His purposes.

✔ Learn to hear from the Lord for yourself; stop depending on others for direction and discernment.

✔ Spend time at His feet. Divine guidance flows out of an intimate relationship with Him.

✔ Allow the seeds of inspiration God plants to come to their full fruit—often growing much bigger than you first think.

✔ Put down your prayer agenda and listen to what the Lord would have you pray.

✔ Trust that what you are seeing or physically sensing is from the Lord, and that there is a purpose behind it. He is big enough to make Himself heard if you are listening, and will confirm as you ask it of Him.

✔ The Lord wants His people to come to an awareness that He knows them, really knows them. Be the messenger.
P.S. Be aware of _your_ feelings—they might not be yours at all.

✔ Be uncomfortable. Be inconvenienced.

✔ Follow through right to the finish that which the Lord sets before you.

✔ Understand that what is happening in the spiritual realm is reflected in the natural realm, and then take appropriate prayer action.

✔ Don't miss the _remarkable_, yet _obvious_ signs. But also be on the lookout for the deeper, hidden ones.

✔ Be patient; the Lord sometimes gives you the answer before you even know the question, rendering it impossible to know what it means at the time. Be ever vigilant; the spiritual realm is more real than the natural one.

✔ God is intentional. Always follow His leading, no matter how subtle.

The Ancient Path

✓ Humbling yourself before the Lord is a rewarding posture.

✓ God exposes our fears so He can heal them. He doesn't want any chinks in our armor.

✓ Pass your tests. Be obedient—even if you don't know or understand the purpose behind what God is asking of you.

✓ Do what it takes to deepen your trust in Him. It is then He can take you to unimaginable heights. The sky is the limit.

✓ Trust the Lord to show you what to pray, how to pray, even if it seems contradictory, out of the ordinary (or perhaps even a little strange).

✓ Don't limit God's plans for you by hanging on to timelines as you understand them to function.

✓ Changing your language opens the door to God's partnership. Answer the call to fast. It changes you—takes you into the depths.

✓ Remain unmoved and ever faithful, even more so in the quiet times.

✔ Prophetic words are blueprints for your journey. Transcribe them. Read them often. Pray into them, declare out of them, and act upon them. (Just don't try to make them happen or put a timeline on them!)

The Ancient Path

CPSIA information can be obtained
at www.ICGtesting.com
Printed in the USA
LVHW080048220120
644356LV00005B/25